TREKKING THE SWISS VIA ALPINA

EAST TO WEST ACROSS SWITZERLAND – THE ALPINE PASS ROUTE

by Kev Reynolds and Jonathan Williams

JUNIPER HOUSE, MURLEY MOSS,
OXENHOLME ROAD, KENDAL, CUMBRIA LA9 7RL
www.cicerone.co.uk

© Jonathan Williams 2023
Fourth edition 2023
ISBN: 978 1 78631 160 3
Third edition 2017
Second edition 2004
First edition 1990

Printed in Singapore by KHL Printing on responsibly sourced paper.
A catalogue record for this book is available from the British Library.

Route mapping by Lovell Johns www.lovelljohns.com.
All photographs are by the author unless otherwise stated.
Contains OpenStreetMap.org data © OpenStreetMap contributors, CC-BY-SA. NASA relief data courtesy of ESRI.

Updates to this Guide

While every effort is made by our authors to ensure the accuracy of guidebooks as they go to print, changes can occur during the lifetime of an edition. Any updates that we know of for this guide will be on the Cicerone website (www.cicerone.co.uk/1160/updates), so please check before planning your trip. We also advise that you check information about such things as transport, accommodation and shops locally. Even rights of way can be altered over time.

The route maps in this guide are derived from publicly available data, databases and crowd-sourced data. As such they have not been through the detailed checking procedures that would generally be applied to a published map from an official mapping agency, although we have reviewed them closely in the light of local knowledge as part of the preparation of this guide. We are always grateful for information about any discrepancies between a guidebook and the facts on the ground, sent by email to updates@cicerone.co.uk or by post to Cicerone, Juniper House, Murley Moss, Oxenholme Road, Kendal, LA9 7RL.

Register your book: To sign up to receive free updates, special offers and GPX files where available, create a Cicerone account and register your purchase via the 'My Account' tab at www.cicerone.co.uk.

Front cover: Looking up to the Blümlisalp range from Kandersteg (Stage 12)

CONTENTS

Symbols used on profiles

⊘ hotel	◉ train station	🐵 refreshments
🡅 mountain hut/inn	◉ bus service	⊕ shop
⊘ campsite	🚠 cable car	❶ information

Symbols used on route maps

Symbol	Description
～	route
⁓ ⁓	alternative route
Ⓢ	start point
Ⓕ	finish point
Ⓢ	alternative start point
Ⓕ	alternative finish point
	glacier
	woodland
	urban areas
	international border
▬■▬	station/railway
▲	peak
)(	pass
⬆	mountain hut/inn
⬡	hotel
🍴	refreshments
⬟	campsite

Relief
in metres

5000 and above
4800–5000
4600–4800
4400–4600
4200–4400
4000–4200
3800–4000
3600–3800
3400–3600
3200–3400
3000–3200
2800–3000
2600–2800
2400–2600
2200–2400
2000–2200
1800–2000
1600–1800
1400–1600
1200–1400
1000–1200
800–1000
600–800
400–600
200–400
0–200

SCALE: 1:100,000

0 kilometres 1 2

0 miles 1

Contour lines are drawn at 50m intervals and highlighted at 200m intervals.

GPX files

GPX files for all routes can be downloaded for free at www.cicerone.co.uk/1160.

ROUTE SUMMARY TABLE

Stage	Start	Finish	High Point
Prologue	Gaflei	Sargans	Gaflei
1	Sargans	Weisstannen	Vermol
2	Weisstannen	Elm	Foopass
3	Elm	Linthal	Richetlipass
4	Linthal	Urnerboden	Fatschbach (nr Nussbüel)
5	Urnerboden	Altdorf	Klausenpass
6	Altdorf	Engelberg	Surenenpass
7	Engelberg	Engstlenalp	Jochpass
8	Engstlenalp	Meiringen	Balmeregghorn
9	Meiringen	Grindelwald	Grosse Scheidegg
10	Grindelwald	Lauterbrunnen	Kleine Scheidegg
11	Lauterbrunnen	Griesalp	Sefinafurgga
12	Griesalp	Kandersteg	Hohtürli
13	Kandersteg	Adelboden	Bunderchrinde
14	Adelboden	Lenk	Hahnenmoospass
15	Lenk	Gstaad	Trütlisbergpass
16	Gstaad	L'Etivaz	Col de Jable
17	L'Etivaz	Rossinière	L'Etivaz
18	Rossinière	Rochers de Naye	Rochers de Naye
19	Rochers de Naye	Montreux	Rochers de Naye
Total (main route)	**Sargans**	**Montreux**	
Total (inc Prologue)	**Gaflei**	**Montreux**	
15A	Lenk	Gsteig	Trütlisbergpass
16A	Gsteig	Col des Mosses	Col des Andérets
Total (alt finish)	**Gaflei**	**Montreux**	

Distance (km)	Ascent (m)	Descent (m)	Time	Page
27	400	1400	7hr	40
13.5	770	250	4hr	46
23	1400	1420	7hr 30min	52
24.5	1550	1880	8hr 45min	59
17.5	1030	300	5hr 30min	65
28	1000	1920	8hr 30min	70
29.5	2040	1500	10hr 30min	78
12	1280	450	5hr	86
22.5	730	1960	7hr	91
23	1500	1060	8hr	98
19.5	1150	1390	6hr 30min	108
22.5	1910	1300	9hr 15min	117
18	1460	1700	7hr 30min	126
17.5	1480	1300	7hr	135
14.0	680	970	4hr 30min	142
22.5	1150	1160	7hr	149
16.5	1170	1080	6hr 30min	156
14.5	300	520	4hr	162
19.0	1900	850	8hr	167
14.0	50	1650	4hr	172
371.5	**22,550**	**22,660**	**129hr**	
398.5	**22,950**	**24,070**	**136hr**	
22.5	1500	1380	8hr	179
25	1470	1210	8hr	179
396	**22,970**	**24,080**	**135hr**	

7

Mountain safety

Every mountain walk has its dangers, and those described in this guidebook are no exception. All who walk or climb in the mountains should recognise this and take responsibility for themselves and their companions along the way. The author and publisher have made every effort to ensure that the information contained in this guide was correct when it went to press, but, except for any liability that cannot be excluded by law, they cannot accept responsibility for any loss, injury or inconvenience sustained by any person using this book.

International distress signal *(emergency only)*
Six blasts on a whistle (and flashes with a torch after dark) spaced evenly for one minute, followed by a minute's pause. Repeat until an answer is received. The response is three signals per minute followed by a minute's pause.

Helicopter rescue
The following signals are used to communicate with a helicopter:

Help needed: raise both arms above head to form a 'Y'

Help not needed: raise one arm above head, extend other arm downward

Emergency telephone numbers
Switzerland: OCVS (Organisation Cantonale Valaisanne de Secours): tel 144

Weather reports
Switzerland: tel 162 (in French, German or Italian), www.meteoschweiz.ch/en

Mountain rescue can be very expensive – be adequately insured.

12 DAYS ON THE TRAIL – A TWO-WEEK TREK

Day	Stage	Time	Distance km	Ascent metres	Descent metres	Transport options
1	Altdorf/Brüsti to Engelberg	6hr 45min	25.9	930	1460	Cable car to Brüsti
2	Engelberg to Engstlenalp	5hr	12.0	1280	450	Cable cars along the route
3	Engstlenalp to Meiringen	7hr	22.5	730	1960	Buses from Engstlenalp, cable car from Planplatten
4	Meiringen to Grindelwald	8hr	23.0	1500	1060	Buses along the route
5	Grindelwald to Wengen	5hr 30min	16.5	1150	920	Cable cars along the route
6	Wengen to Mürren/ Rotstock Hut	5hr 45min	15.3	1320	550	Trains to Lauterbrunnen and Mürren
7	Rotstock Hut to Griesalp	4hr 30min	10.2	590	1220	None
8	Griesalp to Blümlisalp	4hr	6.8	1430	10	None
9	Blümlisalp to Kandersteg	3hr 30min	11.2	30	1690	Cable car from Oeschinensee to Kandersteg
10	Kandersteg to Adelboden	7hr 30min	17.5	1480	1300	None
11	Adelboden to Lenk	4hr 30min	14.0	680	970	Cable cars to Hahnenmoospass
12	Lenk to Gstaad	7hr	22.5	1150	1160	Cable car to Leiterli
Totals		**69hr**	**197.4**	**12,270**	**12,750**	

For a one-week trek, the section of the route from Meiringen to Kandersteg would give the trekker the high section through the Bernese Oberland, sometimes termed the *Bärentrek* (German for Bear Trek) in Switzerland.

Looking down the long valley of the Urner Boden from the climb to the Klausenpass (Stage 5)

PREFACE

The Via Alpina (VA) has now supplanted the Alpine Pass Route (APR) as a journey across Switzerland, giving a fully waymarked Swiss National Trail. This guide reflects this evolution which has been completed in recent years, while seeking to keep the exploratory journey that the original APR provided.

Many major changes were included in the previous (third) edition. These were the start in Liechtenstein, the Planplatten Traverse after Engstlenalp, and the slightly awkward (to plan) stages after Lenk, where the route now heads to Gstaad. This fourth edition now includes the full 'official' finish by way of Lenk–Gstaad–L'Etivaz–Rossinière–Rochers de Naye.

However, after considerable soul-searching we have retained the original finish of Lenk–Lauenen–Gsteig–Col des Mosses–Rochers de Naye as a harder, quicker, more mountainous route for trekkers looking for sterner stuff. There are fewer facilities (likely part of the reasoning behind the official routing) but more of the spirit of a mountain journey. The APR was a route of options, and while we have pruned these back somewhat, we have retained them where they improve the overall experience.

Another change has been in the details of how the route is referenced throughout the guide and we have decided to refer to it as the Via Alpina (VA) rather than the Alpine Pass Route (APR).

One of the results of the codification of the route is that the numbers of Swiss trekkers keen to traverse and explore their country has grown. In time it may come to fulfil the same status as the Coast-to-Coast route in England. Transport in Switzerland is outstanding so taking in a stage or two is easy for many. It is possible to wait for good weather before setting out. Swiss trekkers tend to head in each direction, to the east or the west, and while many would start or finish in Vaduz few seemed interested in walking up or down the Gaflei hill. So, the trail is busier with Swiss walkers as well as international visitors.

However, we have retained the one-way route description from east to west. Montreux with its restaurants, music and transport seems a suitable end point for the international visitor. A small town (or hill) in Liechtenstein does not.

While now a Swiss National Trail, the route remains an outstanding journey across the Alps. It tends to naturally stage from valley to valley, ensuring plentiful accommodation. This limits or restricts to some extent the need and ability to sleep high in refuges and mountain inns; some will appreciate this, others less so. The route is still supported by numerous cable cars, postbuses (distinguished by their yellow paintwork) and regular buses, and mountain trains for those looking to move faster or sustain sore legs.

A question many trekkers have as they consider the route is whether it is a two- or three-week trek? The VA is an exploration of Switzerland's mountains and valleys, and if possible, it should be approached in an open and relaxed manner with ample time allowed. If you want to walk every step of the way it's best to allow closer to three weeks, and the 19 stages plus prologue in Liechtenstein reflect this, giving just under three weeks of walking and allowing for some rest days and bad weather disruptions.

In practice many people will only have time for a two-week trek, and for these the guide suggests ways in which lifts, buses and trains can be used to hold the journey to a comfortable fortnight without detracting from the experience. Postbuses, funiculars, small mountain trains and cable cars are quintessentially part of the Swiss mountain experience, so only the purest of purists would object to their use on this route.

Another option is either tackling the central Oberland *Bärentrek* section – between say Engelberg and Kandersteg (6–7 days) – or splitting into two trips with a break say at Grindelwald or Lauterbrunnen. Other options are considered in the Introduction.

It has been a pleasure to revisit regions we already knew well and to

It's a hard job but someone has to do it – the updating team in action with the Blümlisalp glacier behind (Stage 12)

explore new ones; so what were the highlights? Any long mountain journey has its own routine. Like many such treks in the Alps, the VA has a pass or col almost every day, so the daily routine of early start, climb and descent set the rhythm. Another highlight was the insight gained into the challenges of mountain farming, for Swiss farmers and their cows and sheep manage the landscapes in a way that is both picturesque and accessible. No less interesting were the valleys, villages, resorts and occasional towns along the way.

The 'Oberland giants' took centre stage on the sections between Grindelwald and Mürren, but these in no way diminished the impact of mountains to the east (Tödi, Titlis) and the west (Blümlisalp, Wildstrubel, Les Diablerets). Mountain lakes added to the beauty of the landscapes, while the wildlife – chamois, ibex, marmots – and meadow flowers all contributed to the trekking experience.

On the first day of September we were woken just before seven by the sound of bells – a great many of them, enormous, and ringing at a steady tempo. Viewed through the window of our mountain inn, we were treated to a Swiss ritual as cows descended from their high pasture to the middle levels before their final descent to the lowlands in October. With heads held high, the animals knew it was a special day for them, and they walked past the window at a brisk pace, intent on pastures new. These were their alps, and they knew it. We were merely guests passing through.

Jonathan Williams

Walkers descending near Wengernalp (Stage 10)

INTRODUCTION

Sunset over Lac Léman (Stage 19)

There's immense satisfaction to be gained in undertaking a long journey on foot; especially when that journey takes you among mountains. There's the daily challenge, of course, and rewards when, on reaching the summit of a pass that has occupied most of a morning's effort, you are greeted by a panorama of exquisite beauty, with peaks and ridges far off to lure you on in the days to come. And when at last you gain those distant ridges, you exchange them for yet more new horizons, with new challenges to be met and overcome along the way.

When that journey makes a traverse of the Swiss Alps, with mountains as dramatic as Titlis, Wetterhorn, Eiger, Mönch, Jungfrau, Gspaltenhorn, Blümlisalp and Les Diablerets, it's bound to be a tremendous source of pleasure, bringing a sense of achievement for all who complete it. Such a journey awaits walkers along the Swiss Via Alpina.

THE SWISS VIA ALPINA

For many years the Alpine Pass Route had no official status. However, over recent years it has evolved into the Swiss National Walking Route 1, or the Via Alpina, starting not in Switzerland, but at Gaflei in the Principality of Liechtenstein. From there it passes into Switzerland and through the ancient town of Sargans, the traditional start point, and eventually finds its way to Montreux on the shores of Lac Léman. From Gaflei to Montreux the route

covers just under 400km (250 miles) of mountain and valley, crosses 16 passes and amasses just under 23,000m (75,000ft) of height over 20 stages. Without the Liechtenstein start, saving 27km (17 miles), it would be one day shorter, totalling 370km.

And what a trek it is!

The Liechtenstein section is dealt with here as a prologue to the main route, for it begins outside Switzerland and has no passes to cross. But as it is an essential part of the European Via Alpina network it needs to be included. This 'green trail' is the shortest of the five Via Alpina routes which link all eight Alpine countries through something like 5000km (3100 miles) of footpaths extending from Trieste to Monaco. The shortest it may be, but the Swiss Via Alpina is among the most scenically attractive.

This Liechtenstein prologue takes in a long descent, passing through Vaduz, the Principality's capital, before heading through gentle countryside on the way to Sargans. Here it joins the traditional Alpine Pass Route, now waymarked with the green Via Alpina symbol.

The first full stage of the VA is fairly short as it climbs out of low-lying Sargans and works its way south-westward into a peaceful wooded valley with the half-forgotten village of Weisstannen in which to spend the night. Next day you face a 1200m ascent to the Foopass, a 2223m saddle in a ridge linking the Foostock with Chli- (or Kleine-) Schiben, followed by a long descent to the pretty village of Elm, the highest in the Sernftal, a centre for Swiss geology with an interesting history and a fine outlook.

The Sernftal is blocked by remote-looking ridges, accessed by secluded hanging valleys, and so from Elm the VA leads trekkers onwards into a high pastureland and over the Richetlipass north of the Hausstock. This big mountain overlooks the next valley through which the way descends to Linthal. Like Elm, Linthal is the highest village in its valley, but from there a steep climb takes the route to the car-free resort of Braunwald with its broad views to the Tödi. A gradual descent then draws you into the Urner Boden's vast sweep of cattle-raising pasture topped by the Clariden which guards the Klausenpass.

A scenic road crosses the pass and descends to Altdorf. The VA also goes to Altdorf, but veers away from the Klausenpass road to make a high-level traverse of the northern hillsides.

Altdorf is famed as William Tell's town, and a rather grand statue in the central square commemorates the nation's hero. Nearby lies Attinghausen, a suburb at the foot of a long climb leading to the next col on the list, the delightful 2292m Surenenpass. From here you gain an exciting view of the ice-crowned Titlis, which remains on show for the majority of the descent to Engelberg. It's a glorious route among waterfalls, streams and alp farms, with handsome mountains at every turn.

Looking over the substantial Benedictine monastery in Engelberg at the end of Stage 6

Out of Engelberg the VA twists beneath a cat's-cradle of mechanical lifts before finally reaching the Jochpass, after which it descends to the Engstlensee and the old hotel at Engstlenalp, a favourite with some of the Victorian climbing pioneers. A choice of paths are now on offer for the continuing route to Meiringen; the VA taking a high ridge walk with outliers of the Bernese Alps beckoning, the other options taking lower lines.

Grindelwald is reached by way of an undemanding valley walk below the Engelhörner, before rising to the Grosse Scheidegg, an easy saddle on a spur running north-west from the Wetterhorn. A hotel sits astride the pass, and a private road used by local buses crosses it. Although buses link Meiringen and Grindelwald, plenty of footpath options avoid the road, each

of which presents some of the finest mountain views of the route so far. At the end of the day you can either stay among the crowds in Grindelwald itself, or opt for a remote mountain inn lodged high above the resort with views to hold you spellbound at daybreak.

The walk from Grindelwald to Lauterbrunnen across the Kleine Scheidegg is an almost constant adoration of big mountains – Eiger, Mönch and Jungfrau among them. But Kleine Scheidegg itself is the most cluttered pass of the whole route, and one (despite its views) to leave as quickly as possible. How different is the Sefinafurgga above Mürren! A long climb on grass then shale takes you there, but then you face an extremely steep but well-engineered descent on its western side using fixed cable

17

handrails and timber-braced steps on shifting shale and grit. When at last this relents, a path winds down past isolated farms to a track that eventually deposits you in the little hamlet of Griesalp at the head of the Kiental.

The crossing of the Hohtürli between Griesalp and Kandersteg is one of the most arduous of the VA. At 2778m it's the highest col of the whole route, and a spectacular one at that, and when you emerge from a blinkered ascent among crags that dominate the way, the sudden vista of hanging glaciers, summits and deep valleys is an exciting one. The Blümlisalp Hut stands a short way above the pass and provides the perfect excuse to stop for refreshment before plunging down to Kandersteg, over 1600m below.

Trekking from Kandersteg to Adelboden involves crossing the Bunderchrinde, a narrow slice taken from a craggy ridge, met midway through a day of forest, pasture and scree. It's the final rocky pass of the route, for thereafter grass saddles dominate. From Adelboden there's a fine view of the snowy Wildstrubel, and this remains in view for part of the walk on the next stage to the Hahnenmoos, an invariably busy saddle from which the way continues to Lenk. Neighbouring the Hahnenmoos, the 2055m Pommernpass (Bummerepass on maps) provides an alternative crossing.

The waymarked VA strikes north from the Trütlisbergpass, descending gradually through the Turbach valley into Gstaad, a major resort with apparently some of the best shopping

in Switzerland (though this is unlikely to be of much interest to the lightly loaded trekker!). After this, crossing the easy Col de Jable takes the walker into French-speaking Switzerland with an overnight to be spent in the cheese-making centre of L'Etivaz before a gentle transitional stage through the ballooning centre of Chateau d'Oex to the sleepy village of Rossinière.

However, here the old APR routing has been retained as well, with two passes that are usually tackled on the journey from Lenk to Gsteig. The first of these is the Trütlisbergpass. The second, after briefly visiting Lauenen below the Wildhorn, is the wooded Krinnen Pass, from which the great bulk of Les Diablerets is revealed. Thus far, most of the journey from Sargans has taken the route in a south-westerly direction, but leaving Gsteig you veer away from the long wall of the Bernese Alps and head west, at first twisting up to the little-known Blattipass overlooking the Arnensee. From there the APR takes an undulating course over a pastoral landscape before ending the day at the village of Col des Mosses.

The APR and VA rejoin at the Col de Sonlomont where a high route gives fine views down onto Lac de l'Hongrin, before an unwelcome drop and reclimb to the Col de Chaude and the first views of Lac Léman. An airy ridge route takes in the Rochers de Naye where accommodation is possible (the train service can be of great value at this point if no beds are available). The final stage descends a long ridge with spectacular views to east, west and south, heading down from the Rochers through Caux, Glion and the other-worldly Gorge de Chauderon, from which you emerge in old Montreux, close to the centre of the town.

Above Adelboden the view back is to the big cols of the last few days (Stage 14)

SUGGESTED ITINERARIES

The route has been structured to fit comfortably within three weeks, allowing for bad weather and one or more rest days. However, it is recognised that many walkers may not be able to allow a full three weeks, and previous editions of this guide catered for a demanding two-week trek. For those seeking to complete the route within two weeks, there are many opportunities using postbuses, cable cars and an occasional train to maintain a tighter schedule. As cable cars may only run during the peak summer periods, check in advance before relying on them. Much of the route is very well served by public transport and even if you found yourself apparently marooned at the head of a valley, it is possible to move on a stage by using buses.

Main transport options
- Prologue: Buses between Sargans and Vaduz and Vaduz and Gaflei
- Stage 1: Buses run from Sargans to Weisstannen
- Stage 3: Cable car to Ampächli
- Stage 4: Cable car to Braunwald, postbuses to Urnerboden and Klausenpass
- Stage 5: Postbuses all along the route from Urnerboden to Altdorf
- Stage 6: Cable car to Brüsti
- Stage 7: Cable car to Trübsee and Jochpass, lift to Engstlenalp
- Stage 8: Buses from Engstlenalp to Meiringen, cable cars from Planplatten to Reuti and Meiringen

- Stage 9: Buses from Meiringen to Grindelwald, funicular to the Reichenbach Falls
- Stage 10: Trains over Kleine Scheidegg from Grindelwald to Lauterbrunnen
- Stage 11: Cable car from Lauterbrunnen to Grütschalp, train from Grütschalp to Mürren
- Stage 14: Cable cars up and down the Hahnenmoospass between Adelboden and Lenk
- Stage 15: Betelbahn cable car to Leiterli (off route)
- Stage 16: Cable car to Eggli
- Stage 17: Postbuses between L'Etivaz and Chateau d'Oex and trains to Rossinière,
- Stage 19: Train from Rochers de Naye to Montreux

Not everyone tempted by the VA will feel inclined, or indeed be able, to commit 18–20 or more days of their holiday to an end-to-end trek without the occasional day off. The following suggestions are given for breaking the route into separate walking holidays of a fortnight each.

Sargans to Lauterbrunnen (Stages 1–10), with opportunities to take days off in Engelberg, Meiringen, Grindelwald and Lauterbrunnen to either recuperate or explore the surrounding area. Each resort has a selection of fine walks to enjoy.

Lauterbrunnen to Montreux (Stages 11–18), with days off in Kandersteg, Adelboden, Gstaad, Lauenen or Gsteig. Each of these

Cowbells at the Eggli farm (Stage 16)

villages would repay a wider exploration of their surroundings.

Altdorf to Gstaad (Stages 7–15), with days off in Grindelwald, Lauterbrunnen, Kandersteg, Adelboden, Lenk or Lauenen, Gstaad. See the route outline contained within the 12 days on the trail table.

While the full impact of the VA can only properly be experienced by walking the route in its entirety, it is undoubtedly true that this central section is the most scenically dramatic and rewarding, and in itself makes for a wonderful walking holiday. One or two commercial trekking companies organise holidays – either guided or self-led – along this central part of the VA, which provides an option worth considering.

OPTIONS FOR THE LAST FEW STAGES

As the VA route has been codified, it has in the main followed Cicerone's long-standing APR route. The main exception to this is over the last few stages where a new routing has been established that runs Lenk–Gstaad–L'Etivaz–Chateau d'Oex/Rossinière–Rochers de Naye–Montreux. This compares with the old routing of Lenk–Gsteig–Col des Mosses–Rochers de Naye–Montreux.

There are several differences to note. Firstly, the new VA routing is, for all but the strongest walkers, a day longer. Secondly, the new routing veers into middle- and lower-mountain walking rather than seeking the highest practicable route. Thirdly, the route takes in Gstaad, which is expensive and somewhat discordant

with the feel of most of the rest of the trail. Fourthly, the route seems to go out of its way in an awkward loop, to take in Chateau d'Oex (Stage 17). And lastly, it gives an exposed and unrewarding climb of Les Traverses between Rossinière and the Col de Sonlomont (Stage 18).

It is of course still a great walk, and for those who intend to walk the Via Alpina from start to finish, perfectly satisfactory.

But there are options.

The first notes that a direct route from L'Etivaz to the Col de Sonlomont takes 3hr while that from Rossinière takes 2hr 30min. Effectively an extra day is added that could be 'saved' by 30min walking, so we have retained the option of heading from L'Etivaz directly to Rochers de Naye (see alternative route description, Stage 17) for those who wish to press on through to the finish.

Secondly, and more fundamentally, we have continued to include the 'old' routing from Lenk–Gsteig–Col des Mosses (see Stages 15A and 16A) as this holds its mountain ambiance for longer than the official VA route. It is a day shorter and it remains a fine walk. An easy connecting section rejoins the VA at the Col de Sonlomont.

It rather depends on whether your plan is to walk the Via Alpina route in full, every step of the way, or make a great mountain journey across Switzerland, staying as high and as close to the main mountain 'wall' as possible.

WHEN TO GO

With a number of high or remote passes to cross, it's important to choose the right time to tackle the route. With snow a potential hazard on some of these passes, in a 'normal' year the earliest time to consider setting out would be the beginning of July. Earlier than this and snow and possibly ice could create hazardous conditions on some of the highest and shadiest of places. Even in mid-July it's not unusual to experience patches of soft melting snow; caution is advised if such conditions are encountered.

August is often damp, with sudden storms, while the first half of September is probably the optimum period in which to tackle the route. By late September autumn will be making itself felt, nights will sometimes have a light frost, and accommodation may be difficult to find in some of the smaller villages along the way.

It has to be said that the region traversed by the VA is among the wettest in all Switzerland. The Bernese Alps, for example, attracts banks of unsettled weather which periodically sweep across north-west Europe, and most summers will be marked by days of low cloud and rain, while precipitation can fall as snow at any time on some of the higher passes. However, the mountains are also affected by the warm, dry *Föhn* wind that blows through valleys aligned north to south. Bringing clear skies for several days, in its wake rain should be expected.

In the early summer the VA goes through an extravaganza of flower meadows (Photo: Kev Reynolds)

For up-to-date weather forecasts in Switzerland (in German, French or Italian), consult your preferred app. MeteoSwiss is recommended. Although slightly complex it does a good job in the Swiss mountains.

GETTING THERE – AND BACK AGAIN

By air

The main Swiss airports are at Geneva and Zürich, both of which have numerous scheduled flights from Europe and internationally, with major carriers such as British Airways and SWISS currently dominating the market along with low-cost EasyJet. Ryanair currently flies to Basel. Geneva and Zürich are also the main airports for flights arriving from outside Europe.

Please note that information regarding air travel is especially vulnerable to change. On top of complex fare structures, schedules are often rearranged at short notice, new routes introduced and as quickly cancelled, while airlines come and go (no pun intended) with alarming frequency. The best advice, therefore, is to browse the internet.

While Zürich is the nearest airport to the start of the VA, Geneva is more convenient for the return home after completing the route in Montreux. However, both are accessible by train from almost anywhere in Switzerland in under 4hr, so choose whichever destination is most convenient (or cheaper) for you. Both airports have mainline railway stations, with frequent and dependable services, while Basel airport is a bus ride from the town's railway hub. Sargans

23

The descent from Rochers de Naye keeps to the east of a long ridge (Stage 19)

is on the fast Zürich–Chur line and can be reached in about an hour from Zurich. For Vaduz (Liechtenstein) take the train to Buchs and bus from there.

If coming from Geneva, you will need to allow 4hr 30min for the train journey to Sargans, changing in Zürich. Should you need to return to Zürich (or Basel) on completion of the trek, take the train from Montreux to Lausanne and change there. The journey from Montreux to Geneva is both straightforward and scenic as it runs alongside Lac Léman.

By rail

With a combination of Eurostar (from London's St Pancras station to Paris via the Channel Tunnel) and TGV (Paris to Geneva or Lausanne), high-speed rail travel provides an alternative to flying. On the assumption that connections are met, the overall journey time from London to Geneva can be as little as 8hr, although you should allow about 12hr or more to reach Sargans for the start of the VA.

Currently Eurostar operates trains at least hourly for the 2hr 30min journey between St Pancras International and the Gare du Nord in Paris. On arrival in Paris, it is necessary to transfer to the Gare de Lyon for the TGV departure to either Geneva or Lausanne (the latter station is more convenient for VA travellers), where the journey time is around 3hr 30min.

For a Swiss timetable, go to www. sbb.ch and enter the date and approximate time of travel and journey details. The Swiss Rail app also covers train travel throughout Switzerland and integrates buses, cable cars and even walks across towns.

A range of Europe-wide and Swiss travel passes can provide lower cost travel for those under 25.

Various Swiss passes offer discounted fares on trains, buses, ferries and a number of cableways within Switzerland, but the purchase price (currently 185CHF) is likely to outweigh any savings made by the VA trekker; check the options available by going to www.swiss-pass.ch.

ACCOMMODATION

Happily, there's no shortage of accommodation along the route, for practically every village along the way offers a choice of lodging. This is not limited to centres of habitation, for between villages a mountain inn, farm or hut offering a bed for the night can frequently be found. Some of the most memorable experiences of the VA

often result from a night spent in such comparatively remote places.

Mountain inns along the VA are called a variety of names: *berghof*, *gasthof*, *gasthaus*, *berggasthof* and others. These names appear to be used interchangeably, or with differences so subtle that they are hard to understand. We have sought to use the right version, but sometimes may have not done so. Facilities may vary, but good food and beds are always welcome. Almost universally they are fine establishments where the walker will be made most welcome, an important part of the mountain trekking experience.

One important point to note, however, is that except in resort areas, a number of hotels and inns operate a *ruhetag* – literally a rest day – when they will be closed for a 24hr period. This closed day, where known, is noted

The Berggasthaus at the Jochpass (Stage 7)

in the text. Although like many things Swiss, these days are often stable, be aware that they can and do change.

Outline accommodation details are provided throughout this guide (with website details given where possible) so you can check facilities before leaving home, while telephone numbers are provided to enable you to phone ahead to reserve a bed in a busy season.

Prices are not quoted, as these can change from year to year. While Switzerland has a reputation for being expensive, the budget-conscious trekker will find that costs can be kept down by taking advantage of the numerous *massenlagers* (dormitories) that exist throughout the route. Also known as *matratzenlagers*, literally 'mattress rooms' (*dortoirs* in French), they provide the cheapest option and are frequently available, even in some hotels and mountain inns, as well as on dairy farms and, in some instances, at the upper station of a cableway. Wherever these are known, a note is made in the text. Mixed-sex communal dormitories are the norm, hot showers and meals are usually available, and on rare occasions self-catering facilities are also provided.

Meals may be the costliest items, but if staying overnight in a village it is usually possible to shop around to find a restaurant meal at a reasonable price. Most hotels and inns include breakfast in the price of a bed, while food to eat during the day can be selected from supermarkets along the way.

Mountain huts are mostly situated too far from the route to be of use here, with the exception of the Rotstock Hut above Mürren on Stage 11, and the Blümlisalp Hut which stands a few metres above the Hohtürli on Stage 12. Both are usually open from mid-June until the middle of October. The Rotstock Hut has 45 places, while the SAC-owned Blümlisalp Hut has 130 dormitory places, and during the season both have wardens who provide meals. Members of a recognised Alpine Club can claim a discount on the cost of accommodation, but not meals, at the Blümlisalp Hut.

As for camping, licensed campsites exist in a number of villages and resorts along the VA, but please note that off-site camping is officially prohibited in Switzerland. However, if discreet and pitched well away from habitation, a single overnight in a small tent will usually pass without comment. In my own experience, whenever there was no official campsite available, every farmer approached readily agreed to a request to pitch my tent in a corner of a field and made me most welcome.

Campsites in valleys are noted under the accommodation sections for each stage and are available in (or close to) Vaduz, Sargans, Elm, Linthal, Altdorf, Engelberg, Meiringen, Grindelwald, Lauterbrunnen, Kandersteg, Adelboden, Lenk, Gstaad, Col des Mosses (on alternative route), Chateau d'Oex and Montreux.

LANGUAGES

Making a traverse of Switzerland, the VA travels through two separate language zones. In the east of the country, German (or to be precise, *Schweizerdeutsch*) is used. At L'Etivaz (stage 16), French takes over. Pronunciation of Swiss-German is confused by numerous dialects that can vary from valley to valley and may even be incomprehensible to speakers of High German. On the other hand, French spoken by the Swiss in the western part of the country varies little from more orthodox French.

Although the non-linguistic trekker may have difficulty conversing with the occasional farmer or chamois hunter met along the way, English is widely understood in most places and will almost certainly be spoken by staff in hotels, gasthofs and restaurants, as well as some shops and campsites. If in doubt, a German–French–English glossary is included as Appendix C at the back of this book.

NOTES FOR WALKERS

Despite crossing many high passes, some of which are steep and rugged, the VA demands no technical mountaineering skills of those who tackle it. However, there are occasional short, exposed sections (mostly safeguarded with fixed cable handrail), and a few places where cables and wooden steps aid the ascent to, or descent from, a pass where conditions dictate. Apart from these, the trails are mostly straightforward, albeit with several long stages to be faced.

The upper section of the Hohtürli ascent is sheltered by the rock wall and assisted by wooden steps (Stage 12)

With long days and a number of steep ascents and descents to contend with, it would be sensible to put in some preparation before setting out. Taking regular exercise at home will undoubtedly go some way towards conditioning yourself for the VA's demands, for there's probably no better preparation for a mountain walking holiday than walking – uphill and carrying a rucksack. By putting some effort into getting fit before heading for Switzerland, you'll find that the first pass can be as enjoyable as the last.

Equipment

Unless you plan to camp, backpacking with a large rucksack is unnecessary. With accommodation and meals available on each stage, it's not only possible, but advisable, to trek the VA with a light pack containing little more than the bare essentials and weighing a maximum of 10kg when food and water are included.

Choose your clothing and equipment with care. **Boots**, for example, should be well fitting, lightweight, comfortable and broken in before setting out. They should also have thick cleated soles with plenty of grip. **Waterproofs** are essential, not only for protection against rain, but to double as windproofs. Jacket and trousers made from Goretex (or similar) are recommended, while a lightweight collapsible umbrella can be extremely useful – especially for walkers who wear spectacles.

Some of the passes are more than 2500m (8200ft) high, and can be cold or windy even in summer, so a **fleece** and/or softshell/insulated top should also be taken, plus a warm **hat** and **gloves**. Note that one of the simplest and most effective ways of regulating body temperature is to add or remove your hat and gloves. In addition to protection against wet and cold, be prepared for extremes of sunshine and heat. A **brimmed or peaked hat**, **sun cream** (factor 30 or stronger), **lip salve** and **sunglasses** are essential. Wear **lightweight layers** that can be removed in hot weather.

Take a **first-aid kit**, **water bottle** (minimum capacity 1 litre), **maps**, **compass**, **headtorch** with spare batteries, and a **whistle**. Also, a **penknife** and **emergency food** (it can be replenished every few days), and a **sleeping liner** (a full sleeping bag is not needed) for use in dormitories.

Trekking poles are extremely useful if not critical, especially when descending steep slopes.

Your **rucksack** needs to fit comfortably, with the waist-belt adjusted to take the weight and control any unnecessary movement when walking. A waterproof cover is highly recommended, and a large thick polythene bag in which to pack your gear will safeguard items from getting damp in the event of bad weather. A selection of plastic bags of assorted sizes will be useful.

PATHS AND WAYMARKS

The VA is routed entirely on yellow *Wanderweg* and red/white *Bergwanderweg* mountain paths (see below). For the most part these are clear and obvious, and the Via Alpina signposts, marked with number 1, are close to perfect. The occasional sign might be at a slightly jaunty angle, but the waymarking is generally very strong. Alternative routes described in this book are not waymarked as part of the VA, but are well signed.

Most of the paths adopted by this trek have been in use for centuries by farmers, traders and chamois hunters going about their daily business, from alp to alp, or from one valley to the next. Only in comparatively recent times have they come under the control of local communes or the various cantonal sections of the Swiss Hiking Association (Schweizerische Arbeitsgemeinschaft für Wanderwege), which maintains all official walking routes.

These fall under two main headings: *Wanderweg* and *Bergwanderweg*. The first either remains in a valley, or feeds along a hillside at a modest altitude, and will be well maintained and gently graded. A *Wanderweg* is waymarked with yellow paint flashes, and with metal signposts (also yellow) located in prominent places bearing the names of major landmark destinations, such as a village, pass, lake, alp or footpath junction. The nearest point is shown at the top, the more distant destination at the bottom. Distances are indicated in hours (*Std – Stunden*) and/or minutes (*Min – Minuten*). A small white plate between the yellow direction boards announces the name and altitude at that point.

A *Bergwanderweg* is, literally, a mountain path that ventures higher and is generally more demanding than a *Wanderweg*. It will usually be steeper, rougher, narrower and, sometimes, fading if not in regular use. Exploring the more remote mountain regions, it is waymarked with red and white paint flashes. Signposting is similar to that of the *Wanderweg*, except that the outer section of the finger post will bear red and white stripes. Cairns are occasionally built as additional aids to route-finding where the path fades, or crosses a boulder slope.

A third category of path is the *Alpinwanderweg* or Alpine Trail signed in blue and white and marked

The last sign (Stage 19). Goethe knew what he was talking about: 'you haven't really been there unless you walked'

The Bundschrinde is a narrow cleft in the rocks (Stage 13)

in blue on maps. These are invariably high, steep routes that may require a level of mountaineering skills and equipment, and certainly a head for heights. Some cross glaciers or difficult terrain where it's not possible to create a proper footpath. The VA route and variants do not use blue paths or cross glaciers. The VA is entirely on *Wanderweg* or *Bergwanderweg* paths.

RECOMMENDED MAPS

Swiss mapping is among the best in the world, not only in regard to accuracy, but also in artistic representation. The mapping authority, the Bundesamt für Landestopographie (Office Fédéral de Topographie), publishes three major series of sheets that cover the whole country at 1:100,000, 1:50,000, and 1:25,000,

while the independent publisher Kümmerly & Frey has produced a series of walkers' maps at 1:60,000. All are usually available in the UK from Stanfords or The Map Shop (addresses in Appendix A).

Sheets recommended for the Via Alpina are the 1:50,000 *Wanderkarten*, which are distinguished from the 'standard' sheets published at the same scale by the official Swiss survey by their orange covers and the letter 'T' that accompanies their series number. Details are quoted at the head of each stage of the route described in this book thus: LS (Landeskarte der Schweiz) 247T Sardona.

Clearly the 1:25,000 maps provide greater detail and clarity, but the number of sheets at this scale needed for this particular route would make a bulky load. Given the excellent waymarking on the ground, and detailed

Looking up valley towards Rosenlaui and the Wetterhorn (Stage 9)

route descriptions in this guide, the 1:50,000 sheets should be perfectly adequate for most needs.

Nine LS 1:50,000 sheets (including two double sheets) are required to cover the full route: 237T Walenstadt and 238T Montafon (Prologue and Stage 1); 247T Sardona (Stages 2–3); 246T Klausenpass (Stages 3–5); 245T Stans (Stages 5–6); 255T Sustenpass (Stage 6); 5004 Berner Oberland (Stages 7–10); 5009 Gstaad–Adelboden (Stages 11–14); and 262T Rochers de Naye (Stage 15–18).

The following Kummerley & Frey maps cover the whole route at 1:60,000: 30 Sarganserland (prologue and Stages 1–2); 12 Glarnerland (Stages 3–5); 11 Vierwaldsättersee (Stages 5–6); 19 Gotthard (Stages 7–8); 18 Jungfrau (Stages 9–13); 32 Crans-Montana (Stages 13–15); and 16 Gruyère (Stages 16–18).

Perhaps the most valuable mobile mapping source is the SwissTopo app for iPhone and Android. This gives complete coverage of Switzerland at all scales and allows GPS files to be uploaded. It is preferable to download map tiles in advance in view of the scale of territory covered, as certain remote areas get no phone signal. As a mobile app your position is shown on the screen – this is achieved with data functions turned off, so is gentle on batteries.

Most Swiss LS maps can be downloaded free from the www.schweizmobil.ch website, which also provides a digest of information on Swiss walking and other outdoor activities.

Surrounded by mountains and cliffs, the Oeschinensee is a place to relax after the col (Stage 12)

APPS

In our digital world, apps are a valuable component of the walker's toolkit. Switzerland is covered by many digital mapping resources, such as Outdooractive and PhoneMaps. The following apps are specifically recommended for the walking visitor.

Mapping – The free SwissTopo app provides access to all the Swiss mapping databases, in online and offline (downloadable) formats – note it is important to download the footpath layer. The maps are available in several apps – SwissTopo itself and SwitzerlandMobility are just two.

Travel – SBB is a complete travel app for Swiss trains, buses and connecting cable cars, as well as some other services. The app brings together the entirety of the Swiss public transport system into a seamless whole. It's easy to use, linking with online payments and storing a Swiss Travel Pass if you have applied for this as well. Note that if you have any type of discount card, you will need to show a printout (even if you have an e-ticket) when tickets are inspected.

Weather – MeteoSwiss is a weather app from the Swiss meteorological agency that has full forecasting capabilities. It takes a little time to get the hang of, as it has lots of resources to explore, but it's worth the effort and is a bit more accurate than more general weather apps that don't fully account for Swiss mountain conditions.

SAFETY IN THE MOUNTAINS

Although the VA is well signed and waymarked, and working farms and villages are strung along the route, there are several remote sections where an accident could have serious consequences. Mountains contain a variety of objective dangers for the unwary, and while the vast majority of walkers who set out will complete the route without anything untoward happening, all should be prepared to cope with any hazards that might arise. The following list of dos and don'ts are merely common-sense suggestions based on years of experience and are offered as a means of avoiding mishaps. With a little attention to detail, the chances are that you'll experience nothing more distressing than a small blister.

Planning tips
- Plan each day's stage with care. Study the route outline, height gain and loss, and the estimated time to reach your destination.
- Make sure you have sufficient hours of daylight in which to cross the pass and descend to the safety of the next night's lodging – this is especially important late in the season when days are shorter.
- Don't over-estimate your physical ability, but make an allowance for delays and interruptions, for bad weather and imperfect trail conditions.

- Check the weather forecast before setting out. This is often posted at tourist offices, although your hotel or gasthof owner will probably be able to advise.
- Inform a responsible person (hotel receptionist, hut warden) of your intended route, and stick to it wherever possible.
- Carry an up-to-date topographical map and compass – and know how to use them.
- Carry a mobile phone and make sure it is fully charged. Download the Rega helicopter rescue app and Swiss144 app (an insurance rescue card that covers search, rescue and first aid costs and links to the emergency services).
- Keep to approved paths and avoid taking short cuts.
- Consult the map frequently and anticipate any obstacles or changes of direction.
- Do not stray from the path in foggy conditions.
- Keep alert for signs of deteriorating weather, and don't be too proud to turn back should it be safer to do so than continue in the face of an oncoming storm, or along a trail that has become unjustifiably dangerous.
- Don't venture onto exposed ridges or passes if a storm or high wind is imminent.
- Should you be overtaken by an electric storm, avoid prominent rocks, isolated trees and metallic objects, and discard trekking

poles and umbrellas. Do not shelter in caves, beneath overhanging rocks or in gullies. Instead, kneel or squat on your rucksack with head down and hands on knees.

- For UK trekkers a GHIC (formerly EHIC) card will ensure reimbursement of most medical costs. But travel and rescue insurance is still recommended. European trekkers will have EHIC cover.

If you have an accident

- In the unhappy event of an accident, stay calm. Move yourself and the injured person (if feasible, and with care not to aggravate the injury) away from any imminent danger of stonefall or avalanche and apply immediate first aid. Keep the victim warm, using any spare clothes available.

- Make a written note of the precise location where the victim can be found, and either telephone for assistance using a mobile phone (if you can get a signal) or send for help while someone remains with the injured member – assuming, that is, you're in a party of more than two people. Should a mountain hut or farm be nearby, seek assistance there. If valley habitation is nearer, find a telephone and dial **tel 112 Emergency number** or **tel 1414 Helicopter rescue** (but note the latter should only be used if absolutely essential) or use a rescue app such as Swiss144.

- Remember, there is no free rescue service in Switzerland and no free hospital treatment. The cost of an emergency could therefore be extremely expensive. Be

Parting clouds show the route over Grat Alp and back to the mountains around the Klausenpass (Stage 6)

adequately insured and be cautious. (It is advisable to leave a copy of your travel itinerary and insurance details with a responsible person at home, and to carry with you photocopies of important documents – information pages of your passport, insurance certificate, travel tickets and so on – as well as an emergency home contact address and telephone number.)

USING THIS GUIDE

The route is described heading in a south-westerly direction and is broken into 19 stages (plus a prologue in Liechtenstein), each of which equates to a day's travel. Some of these are very long, but they could either be interrupted by spending a night between stages or shortened by use of public transport. Wherever options occur, they are mentioned in the text. The itinerary given in this guidebook is certainly not the only one possible, for with accommodation listed as and where it is found along the route, readers are encouraged to suit their personal requirements. The Route summary table and Stage facilities planner (see Appendix D) will assist in creating itineraries that meet your trekking needs. A 2-week/12-day suggestion is also given in the 12 days on the trail itinerary.

Each stage described is accompanied by a map showing the route. These are not intended as an alternative to the topographical maps listed at the head of each stage, but should be used in conjunction with them. A route profile is also given, which shows the main ups and downs of each stage, as well as the facilities available along the way (see 'Symbols used on profiles' key).

At the beginning of each stage description, a summary of the day's route is given in terms of distance, approximate time needed to reach the day's destination, height gain and loss, and so on. Heights and distances are given throughout in metres and kilometres.

Distances have been measured and cross-checked by GPS. Heights are referenced to the SwissTopo online maps (as the latest measures), and also heights stated on signposts, where relevant. Swiss mappers continually improve their measures and accuracy, so there are often very small height differences (1–3m) between maps of various vintages and types, and also the yellow signs (which tend to catch up with maps over the years).

Since most trekkers measure their progress by the amount of time that they take to walk from point A to point B, it is important to remember that times quoted in this guide are approximations only, and make no allowances for rest stops, photographic interruptions or consultations with the guidebook or map. Add a factor for these and adjust for whether your walking times are faster or slower than guidebook time.

A colourful chalet on the path up towards the Reichenbach Falls (Stage 9)

Inevitably times quoted here will be considered fast by some walkers, slow by others, but by comparing your own times with those given in the text you will soon discover by how much your pace differs and make the necessary adjustments. The route has been designed for maximum enjoyment of the mountain world, and this guidebook reflects that aim, so in order to get the most out of your experience of the VA don't be tempted to hurry (unless the weather dictates otherwise).

Throughout the text, route directions 'left' and 'right' refer to the direction of travel, whether in ascent, descent or hillside traverse. However, when used with reference to the banks of rivers or glaciers, 'left' and 'right' refer to the direction of flow, ie, down-valley. Where doubts might occur, a compass direction is also given.

Specific features or items of interest mentioned are described in more detail in boxes or in the sidebar within the route stage. Alternative route options which trekkers may consider that diverge from the official VA route are clearly flagged.

Abbreviations are used sparingly, but some have of necessity been adopted. While most should be easily understood, the following list is given for clarification:

APR	Alpine Pass Route
hr	hours
km	kilometres
K&F	Kümmerly & Frey (maps)

The rooftops of Glion; it feels as though you are nearly there but the VA has a final challenge before Montreux is reached (Stage 19)

LS	Landeskarte der Schweiz (Swiss survey maps)
m	metres (height)
min	minutes
SAC	Swiss Alpine Club
TGV	Trains à Grande Vitesse (the superfast French train)
VA	Via Alpina

GPX tracks

GPX tracks for the routes in this guidebook are available to download free at www.cicerone.co.uk/1160/GPX. A GPS device is an excellent aid to navigation, but you should also carry a map and compass and know how to use them. GPX files are provided in good faith and are accurate for the general purpose for which they have been recorded – mountain walking following marked paths. If following GPX tracks you should always consider their accuracy – especially taking into consideration the steep terrain – assess likely danger areas and take due care in any situation you find yourself in.

INFORMATION AT A GLANCE

Currency Swiss franc (CHF); 100 centimes/rappen = CHF1. Although Switzerland is not in the Euro zone, some hotels and retail outlets accept Euros, but change will be given in Swiss francs. Most credit cards are acceptable as a means of payment in many hotels and gasthofs along the VA, but it's advisable to carry cash. In larger villages/resorts there are banks with ATMs (cash machines). Banks are usually open Monday to Friday 8.30am–4.30pm. Most international cards work in ATMs but occasionally in remote parts of the country it may be necessary to identify in person with a passport.

Formalities Many or most international travellers do not require a visa to enter Switzerland, but check in advance. Citizens of the USA, Canada, Australia, New Zealand and South Africa can stay for up to three months without a visa. UK citizens are also subject to the EU/Schengen visiting restrictions of 90 days in any 180-day period. Changes to EU entry requirements may be reflected in Switzerland – although Switzerland is not an EU member, it is part of the common travel area.

Health precautions At the time of writing there are neither major health concerns to consider nor vaccinations required by visitors from Europe and the West. However, there is no free health care in Switzerland. UK travellers should take GHIC/EHIC cards. It is also advisable to take out insurance cover that includes personal accident and sickness, and obtain mountain rescue cover through the British Mountaineering Council or by joining the Austrian Alpine Club or similar national organisation.

COVID Check COVID regulations carefully before travelling. At the time of writing measures against the virus have largely been lifted, but the situation may change. Also check the regulations for other countries you may be visiting and returning to.

International dialling code When calling Switzerland from the UK, use: 0041. To phone the UK from Switzerland the code is 0044, after which you ignore the initial 0 of the area code that follows. Mobile phone coverage is mostly excellent, certainly in the valleys. It is usually excellent in the mountains too, but there are occasional gaps in coverage.

Languages Both German and French are spoken along the VA; German (*Schweizerdeutsch*) on Stages 1–15, and French after Gstaad/Gsteig to Montreux, but English is widely understood almost everywhere in hotels, shops and restaurants.

Tourist information Switzerland Travel Centre Ltd, 8 Floor, Saint Clare House, 30–33 Minories, London, EC3N 1DD (www.switzerlandtravelcentre.com/en/gbr).

THE SWISS VIA
ALPINA

The Oeschinsee lake (Stage 12)

THE LIECHTENSTEIN START

PROLOGUE
Gaflei to Sargans

Start	Gaflei 1483m
Finish	Sargans 483m
Distance	27km
Total ascent	400m
Total descent	1400m
Time	7hr
High point(s)	Gaflei 1483m
Maps	LS 237T Walenstadt and 238T Montafon; K&F 30 Sarganserland
Transport	Bus (Gaflei–Vaduz, Vaduz–Sargans). Regular buses from Vaduz to Gaflei take 30min.
Accommodation	Sücka (off route), Vaduz, Sevelen, Azmoos, Sargans (see Sargans below)

Starting an almost three-week traverse of Switzerland's passes with a long downhill in another country does have a slightly counter-intuitive feel, but the descent through the woods is interesting, while the countryside after the covered wooden Rhine bridge is decidedly bucolic. Vaduz feels like a small Swiss town except its buses are a different shade of yellow, and with few signs of the busy tax accountants for which Liechtenstein is renowned.

It would be possible to stay in Sargans for two nights, taking the bus to Vaduz or Gaflei. Walking from Vaduz to Weisstannen in a single day would be a 9hr walk, perhaps too much for a first stage.

THE VIA ALPINA IN LIECHTENSTEIN

The official Swiss Via Alpina starts at Gaflei, a spa hamlet and car park in Liechtenstein, dropping down through Vaduz, the capital of the Principality, crossing the Rhine and then on to Sargans where the APR has traditionally started.

Slightly confusingly the European Via Alpina red route also passes close by Gaflei, and can be joined with the VA either by a short descent to Gaflei, or a 1hr 30min walk from Sücka where stage 57 of the red route ends. Sücka can be reached from Vaduz by bus, getting off at Steg and walking 10min to Sücka, where there is accommodation at Berggasthaus Sücka.

The red Via Alpina route takes a different route through Switzerland and joins the Swiss Via Alpina for a stage before diverging again at the Trütlisbergpass above Lenk (Stage 15), from where it makes its way southwards to the Mediterranean at Monaco.

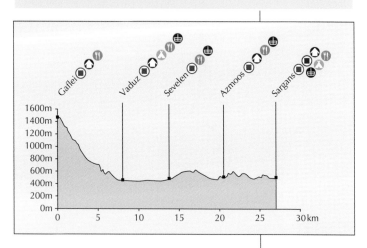

From the entrance to the car park at **Gaflei** take the signed track downhill, watching for a left turn after 250 metres. It starts unpromisingly through pasture, but is signed with a marker post in the field. Pass below a viewing platform (reached by passing the left turn). From here the route drops steeply to the left. ▶

In places during the first half hour the route can be steep, narrow, muddy and potentially slippery, living up to its Bergweg sign.

After 30min cross another trail, and after 60min and 600m of descent come to a clearing and the entrance to the **Wildschloss**. This is the ruined Schalun Castle which started falling down as early as 1200AD. Follow the forest track, which is signed at the start but has limited signage until you reach the outskirts of Vaduz after many zigzags and 1000m of downhill.

Turn left at the first houses (Letzi) then pass **Vaduz Castle**, turn right along the road and at the second bend take the waymarked path dropping steeply into the town. The path is decorated with boards explaining the history of the Principality, and it drops you at a plaza in the centre of **Vaduz** (457m, **2hr 15min**, restaurants, accommodation, bars, cafés, shops, banks). Cross the plaza and at the roundabout turn right and then left (although straight across and then right works just as well).

Vaduz Castle occupies a prominent position 120m above the town to which it gave its name. Thought to have been built as a fortress in the 12th century, the castle became properly habitable as early as 1287, and was acquired by the Princely Family in 1712.

Vaduz Castle in Liechtenstein

Following a long period of decline, it was restored by Prince Franz Joseph in 1939 and adopted as the official residence of the Liechtenstein Royal Family, which it remains to this day (see www.tourismus.li).

From the town centre the official route takes a 2–3km detour through the attractive meadowland of Haberfeld to the north before turning south parallel to the Rhine and passing Vaduz football stadium, a smart modern affair. It is straightforward to cut this loop, and from the town centre you head straight towards the river, joining the trail just before the Rhine bridges.

Cross the elegant, covered cyclepath and footbridge, completely made from wood, and pass into Switzerland (**3hr**). Turn left then right at the road bridge, then left after a road junction along an irrigation channel then right and into **Sevelen** (471m, **3hr 50min**). ◄

The land is pancake flat, and although Sevelen is industrial (home to Schoeller, makers of fabrics widely used in outdoor and work clothing), the upper part is a much more traditional Swiss village with a fine church.

In the centre of the village turn left along a road with a bar on the corner heading south-west. The signs suggest around 4hr to Sargans, but in fact it's nearer three. The track climbs steadily and after 20min and 100m of ascent turn left on a path signed to Azmoos. Passing through woods and pastures, with better and better views as you climb, pass the ruined castle near Wartau and reach the

Castle on the route between Sevelen and Sargans

village of **Gretschins**. Turn left along the road and then right at the bus stop. Descending, the path makes a sharp left turn by an attractive cottage and drops alongside a small stream that has gouged an impressively deep gorge. At the hamlet of **Fontnas** cross a bridge and turn left along a road which enters the straggling village of **Azmoos**; 1hr 30min from Sevelen (gasthaus, accommodation, food).

At the large hexagonal water fountain turn right and walk uphill through attractive older houses on a narrow street. The road turns into a track through pastures, and crosses beneath a small hill (the Maxiferchopf) looking down over the Rhine, motorway and flat valley bottom with views to the Rätikon Alps and beyond.

Descending to the road at Vild, the route appears to be entering Sargans, but it is merely teasing and the route (perhaps disappointingly if this is late in the day) heads back uphill past a restaurant built into an old mine gallery, signed to Sargans 45min. The road turns into a track, and then a smaller and smaller grassy path heading in the direction of Sargans Castle, seen ahead. Turn right up the short stretch of road immediately before the castle and then descend left through the grounds, pass a chapel and quite suddenly you come out on the main road in the middle of **Sargans** (483m, **7hr**). Having done it, you may well think that the longer route into town was worth the extra effort. Details on transport and accommodation for Sargans are given in Stage 1.

The Rätikon Alps form a fine backdrop to the descent into Sargans

THE MAIN ROUTE

STAGE 1
Sargans to Weisstannen

Start	Sargans 483m
Finish	Weisstannen 1004m
Distance	13.5km
Total ascent	770m
Total descent	250m
Time	4hr
High point(s)	Vermol 1030m
Maps	LS 237T Walenstadt; K&F 30 Sarganserland
Transport	Postbus (Sargans–Schwendi–Weisstannen)
Accommodation	Sargans – hotels, gasthofs; Mels (30min) – hotels; Weisstannen – hotels

This first stage is both short and undemanding, giving an opportunity to ease gently into the long walk to come. Breaking away from the low, flat valley of the Seeztal, it climbs into the wooded Weisstannental to the southwest, and makes an ideal introduction, putting walkers in a good position to tackle the first pass of the route the following day. If you overnighted in Sargans it makes a pleasant short day, and could be extended to Alp Vorsiez, shortening Stage 2 by an hour.

The Weisstannental is distinctly pastoral, with woods clothing the lower hillsides that occasionally spill across the valley floor. At its entrance, behind Mels, the valley is squeezed into a tight defile, forcing the route along its western flank. The walk then goes through woodland and across open pastures to gain its highest point near the little alp hamlet of Vermol. It then eases slowly down to river level at Schwendi, where it crosses to the east side of the river and meanders gently uphill to Weisstannen. Alternatively take a higher path on the west bank at Schwendi (signed Windegg) among more trees and meadows.

SARGANS (483M)

Sargans is a small ancient town at the confluence of the Seeztal and the Rhine's valley where the latter breaks northward alongside Liechtenstein. Just outside the town to the north, the site of a Roman city was discovered in 1967. Of more recent origin, the old castle (*Schloss*) that commands the town was built for the Counts of Toggenburg between the 13th and 15th centuries. There is a museum of local life and history in the castle. Rising above the town is the steep little peak of Gonzen (1830m), whose ascent is made by footpath from Sargans in around 4hr, and whose summit gives a splendid panoramic view which includes the Walensee and the Rhine Valley from Landquart to the Lake of Constance – but of special interest to VA walkers is the view south-westward into the Weisstannental. Local tourist information promotes Sargans as the centre of 'Heidiland', and indeed the countryside is beautiful.

Tourist information (www.sargans-tourismus.ch). Hotels, gasthofs, restaurants, shops, PTT, railway station (Zürich–Chur). If needed, the bus to Weisstannen leaves from the railway station. Accommodation includes: Mariandl's Bed & Breakfast located on Zürcherstrasse (tel 081 723 42 20, www.mariandlsbnb.ch). Also in Zürcherstrasse there's Hotel & Restaurant Garni Franz Anton (tel 081 723 30 35, www.hotelfranzanton.ch), while the Bahnhofstrasse is where you'll find Hotel Post (tel 081 720 47 47, www.hotelpost-sargans.ch), Hotel Déjà & Pub (tel 076 461 97 93) and Hotel zum Ritterhof (tel 081 710 68 30, www.hotel-ritterhof.ch).

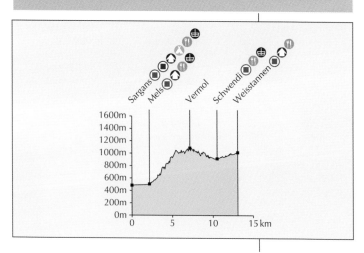

Through gaps between the houses you have views of a fine onion-domed church and the town's stately castle backed by the steep crags of the Gonzen.

On leaving the railway station in **Sargans** walk along the road beside the railway heading in a north-westerly direction (towards the town centre) until you reach Hotel Zum Ritterhof. Here you take a tarmac footpath, the Bahnweg, between the railway & the hotel, which continues behind a row of houses. ◄

At the end of the tarmac path go down a few steps to a road and turn left to pass beneath a bridge carrying the railway and a road. Turn left at the roundabout and then right at the next junction on Schwarzackerstrasse, follow this street as it bears right and then turn left in Sarganserstrasse. Continue to Wangserstrasse and turn right into the centre of **Mels** (495m, **35mins**). Mels monastery is to the left here.

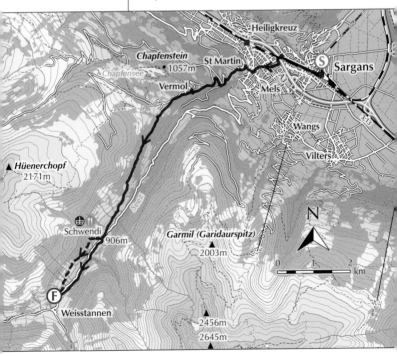

Mels offers tourist information (www.mels.ch), hotel, B&B, refreshments, shops, post office, postbus. Hotel Schweizerhof (tel 081 723 12 44, www.hotel.schweizerhof-mels.ch).

The attractive Seiz bridge in the village of Mels about 40min after setting off from Sargans

The heart of Mels, whose parish church dates from the 9th century, is an attractive place with a number of fine buildings. On coming to the village square with its fountain, head across (sign to Vermol) to cross the River Seez which comes bursting from the Weisstannental. About 3min after crossing the bridge, cut sharply left up the steeply climbing Burggasse, taking you between houses and eventually bringing you back onto the road which has made a loop up the hillside. Moments later enter the hamlet of **St Martin** (572m, **45min**).

Immediately after passing a small chapel the road forks. Take the left branch to find yourself above a steep slope of vineyards, with good views stretching across the rooftops of Mels to Sargans and the valleys of the Rhine and the Seez, to the mountains of Liechtenstein, and the wave-like crest of the Churfirsten above the unseen Walensee, the lake you almost certainly passed on the way to Sargans.

The small chapel in St Martin, just above Mels

A few metres beyond the first hairpin bend leave the road on a *Wanderweg* path which breaks away to the left and climbs steeply through mixed woodland. Climb on an old mule track, sometimes crossing and sometimes joining the road, but always ascending. Pass the turn signed to Chapfensee lake, taking the left turn signed to Vermol, Schwendi and Weisstannen. The track continues through the woods, and finally leaves the road at the Güetli junction (914m, **1hr 40min**). Keep left and continue climbing to a junction of tracks marked as Tschess (1020m, **1hr 40min**). The houses of upper Vermol can just be seen above.

Take the left-hand option which goes downhill a little, and then comes out of the woods on the lower edge of **Vermol**. The way then continues as a gradually descending hillside traverse. Ignore the path which breaks off left at Hundbüel (1000m, **2hr**) and continue on the unmetalled road which is signed to Schwendi and Weisstannen. The track becomes a path, in one place descending steeply on a tricky staircase of roots, and continues to undulate through woods and hay meadows, some steep, joining a metalled farm road leading to the string of barns and farms at **Schwendi** (906m, **3hr 15min**, foodstore, water supply, restaurant (Gasthaus Mühle)).

Here come onto the valley road and turn left after 100 metres. The VA route takes a riverside path on the east side of the Seez from Schwendi to Weisstannen. There are other options for the continuing walk to Weisstannen, all of which take about 45min; the second route takes a track on the right near Gasthaus zur Mühle, then follows a path through meadow and woodland passing Windegg;

View up the Seez valley from the path after Vermol

thirdly it is possible to walk directly up the quiet road to
Weisstannen (1004m, **4hr**).

WEISSTANNEN (1004M)

This peaceful 'back-of-beyond' village is set in an attractive location a little over
halfway along its valley. It's a modest farming community, with the smell of cows
and haymaking everywhere. A number of the buildings are typical of the region
and are heavily reliant on timber for their construction. The small church, dedicated to St John the Baptist, dates from 1665. Weisstannen has a post office and a
school, and is served by postbus from Sargans.

Accommodation at Hotel Gemse (closed Tuesday and Wednesday, tel 081 723
17 05, www.weisstannen.ch), and Hotel Alpenhof (tel 081 723 17 63, www.
alpenhof-weisstannen.ch).

STAGE 2
Weisstannen to Elm by the Foopass

Start	Weisstannen 1004m
Finish	Elm 979m
Distance	23km
Total ascent	1400m
Total descent	1420m
Time	7hr 30min
High point(s)	Foopass 2223m
Maps	LS 247T Sardona; K&F 30 Sarganserland
Transport	Bus (Weisstannen–Alp Vorsiez)
Accommodation	Alp Vorsiez (1hr 10min) – dormitory accommodation; Elm – hotels, gasthofs, pensions, camping

The crossing of the Foopass is symbolic, for with over 1200m of ascent required to gain it (and even more to descend from it) the true nature of the Via Alpina is revealed. Once this pass is behind you, you'll be left in no doubt as to what lies ahead in the days to come. It's also worth noting that the route to Elm takes you through the heart of the Geopark Sardona (otherwise known as the Swiss Tectonic Arena Sardona).

The day begins easily enough with about 8km of walking on paths and tracks alongside the river, with the option of taking the road for a faster start if you want to conserve your energy for the climb to the pass. This begins from the roadhead, and although steep in places, the way is clearly defined as far as Fooalp. From there it continues without difficulty, meandering over high pastures before tackling the final ascent. The Foopass marks the canton border between St Gallen and Glarus, and views ahead offer a foretaste of what is to come. The initial descent on the western side of the pass is steep, but this eventually eases for a pleasant walk down to Elm, mainly on good tracks.

Follow the road out of **Weisstannen** and then cross the river, taking a path that follows the riverside upvalley. The valley here is heavily wooded, opening now and again to pastureland, while the mountains ahead gather in a neat

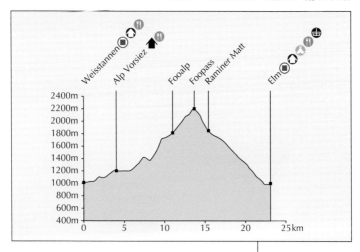

amphitheatre. Waterfalls and streams drain the steep hill-sides and feed into the Seez, which flows parallel to the road. The path passes several birdwatching platforms and joins the road for a while before heading off left, climbing above the river only to descend later.

After an hour you will see the farms at Alp Vorseiz below you. Cross a metal footbridge over the Heubützlibach, close to the point where it flows into the Seez, and rejoin the road near the farm of **Vorsiez** (1175m, **1hr 10min**).

> **Alp Vorsiez** Refreshments, rooms and 35 dormitory places (tel 081 723 17 48, www.alpsiez.ch). Closed Sundays.

Join a farm track a few paces downstream of Alp Vorsiez. This route then angles upvalley for 1.5km before forking left and sloping downhill. Continue straight ahead at a hairpin in the trail and continue through woods, climbing to join a higher trail. ▶ Continue across pastures to join the roadhead at **Untersäss** (1359m, **2hr 10min**).

A well-placed water trough provides a welcome break.

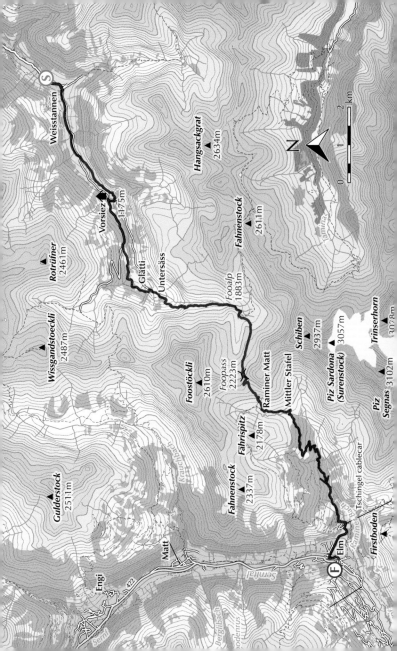

Weisstannen

Rotrüfner
2461m

Vorsiez
1175m

Wissgandstoeckli
2487m

Glätti

Untersäss

Hangsackgrat
2634m

Fahnenstock
2611m

Fooalp
1883m

Gulderstock
2511m

Foostöckli
2610m

Foopass
2223m

Schiben
2937m

Piz Sardona
(Surenstock)
3057m

Trinserhorn
3028m

Raminer Matt

Mittler Stafel

Piz
Segnas
3102m

Fahnenstock
2337m

Fährispitz
2178m

Matt

Engi

Tschingel cablecar

Elm

Firstboden

S

F

N

0   1   2 km

Alternatively, from Alp Vorseiz, it is possible to stay on the road which keeps to the south bank of the river. A short distance beyond Glätti the road crosses the Seez and brings you to the roadhead at Untersäss.

Looking back down the valley to Untersäss

Now leave the road and cross a stream, aiming towards the head of the valley. Watch for a right-hand turn with red and white waymarks directing a path that climbs up and across an area of rockfall, then among shrubs with occasional views back down through the valley where the Weisstannental is a long green shaft darkened by thick woods.

Making a steady but steep ascent on a well-graded but remarkably stony path, the route is brightened not only by shrubs on the hillsides but by waterfalls cascading ahead. It's a stern climb for 300m, coming out at a fine viewpoint and bench. ▶ The path follows the stream for about 1km, before turning right and then climbing a steep stone staircase protected by a cable, at the top of which you emerge at **Fooalp** (1883m, **3hr 45min**) – a solitary farm and a cattle byre by another steam, the Foobach.

The viewpoint comes just after passing a sign for Urnerboden, still two days ahead, painted optimistically on a rock.

Above the farm cross the stream then climb to a signed junction and bear right and climb across more rough pastureland inhabited by marmots and patrolled

55

by cattle, moving over occasional boggy patches, then across a flatter section and finally up a grassy rib before easing towards the **Foopass** (2223m, **4hr 45min**).

The **Foopass** is a slender saddle in the ridge which links the Foostock with the Surenstock (Piz Sardona). It's an effective divide that carries the cantonal boundary, and its crossing leads to a fresh landscape hinting of fine things to come.

On the western side the path drops steeply at first in zigzags, then more gently, and about 30min from the pass you reach the alp building of **Raminer Matt** (1898m, **5hr 15min**, possible refreshments). Turn left along a farm track, and 15min later come to a second alp, **Mittler Stafel** (1759m). Now turn right and descend on the track, taking a left fork onto a less-used track. There are good views to enjoy as you work down through forest and alongside meadows, crossing side streams and with occasional views across the valley to the slopes of the Tschingelhoren and back to the snow-capped Piz Sardona, with waterfalls streaking the hills and green meadows drawing you on.

After crossing a meadow, enter woodland and continue on a good but little-waymarked track, descending steadily through thicker forest to a hairpin junction with

a road. Continue down the road, and after 5min take a small left hand turn below the road. This cuts out one hairpin. Then follow another path that drops steeply to the roadhead by the Tschingelhoren cable car station. Continue on the road past the campsite of Zeltplatz Wisli. A route to Elm is signed left, but the VA keeps to the road descending to **Elm** (979m, **7hr 30min**).

The snow-capped Piz Sardona and its geologically complex structure

ELM (979M)

The attractive, strung-out village of Elm provides an opportunity to stock up with supplies for the onward journey, for among its shops there is a supermarket and a bakery. Its houses are neat and flower-decked, including the Suworowhaus named for the Russian general who stayed there in 1799 (see box below). The village lies at the heart of the so-called Geopark Sardona (a UNESCO World Heritage Site) which contains the 'Glarus Thrust' that is most evident on Piz Sardona to the east of Elm. Following the ridge to the south-west, the well-known Martinsloch is a clearly visible hole in the rock, through which, just after daybreak, the sun shines on two days a year (12/13 March and 30 September/1 October) to beam onto the tower of the 15th-century church. Trim meadows spread beyond the village and give no hint of the tragedy that struck on Sunday 11 September 1881, when a steep 500m rock buttress known as the Plattenbergkopf, which for 13 years had been quarried for slate, suddenly collapsed on the village killing 114 people. (RLG Irving's book, *The Alps* [Batsford, 1939] contains a graphic account of this tragedy.) Upvalley can be seen the Glarner and Bündner Vorab, and the 3158m Hausstock whose ridges enclose the valley's head.

Tourist information (tel 055 642 52 52, www.elm.ch). Camping, restaurants, banks, shops, post office, buses. Accommodation: simple dorms at the Gemeindehaus Touristenlager (tel 055 642 17 41, www.gemeindehaus-elm.ch); standard rooms at Gasthaus Sonne (closed Wednesday, tel 055 642 12 32, www.sonne-elm.ch), Gasthaus Segnes (10 rooms, tel 055 642 11 72, www.segnes.ch), Hotel Elmer (40 beds, tel 055 642 12 20, www.hotelelmer.ch), and on the road to Erbsalp on Stage 3, there's Hotel Zum Bergführer (closed Tuesday, tel 055 642 21 06, www.hotelbergfuehrer.ch).

SUWOROW'S MARCH

The Suworow Haus stands in the main street in Elm, with a plaque on the wall celebrating the Russian general who stayed there in 1799 on his retreat from a series of battles with Napoleon's forces.

General Alexander Suworow (or Suvorov) was 70 years old and living in retirement in Moscow when he was recalled by the Russian Emperor and dispatched to Italy to help the Austrians against the French. Winning three quick battles he was then ordered to Switzerland to aid General Korsakoff in his attempt to drive back more of Napoleon's men. It was September when Suworow and his 22,000 battle-weary soldiers marched across the St Gotthard Pass, only to be met with fierce opposition in the Schöllenen Gorge where the French were lying in wait. A heavy three-day battle ensued, and on the night of the 27th the French destroyed the Devil's Bridge and retreated. The Russians pushed on down to Altdorf and Flüelen on the Vierwaldstättersee (Lake Lucerne), but as the French had seized all the boats Suworow was forced to change direction, crossing the Chinzig Chulm (near the Klausenpass) and descending into the Muotatal. Once more the French were waiting and the Russians were forced into combat again on 1 October before turning east, and fighting their way over the Pragel Pass to Glarus. Here again the French blocked their way, so Suworow turned south up the valley that leads to Elm. A night was spent there, then they continued upvalley to cross the 2407m Panixer Pass between the 6th and 8th, where the remnants of his army were caught in a blizzard as they descended above Alp di Pigniu. Hundreds of exhausted Russian soldiers fell to their deaths, as did countless pack animals. Five days later, when they finally crossed into Austria to reach the remains of Korsakoff's army, just 14,000 of Suworow's men had survived the long march.

STAGE 3

Elm to Linthal by the Richetlipass

Start	Elm 979m
Finish	Linthal 650m
Distance	24.5km
Total ascent	1550m
Total descent	1880m
Time	8hr 45min
High point(s)	Erbser saddle 2161m and Richetlipass 2261m
Maps	LS 247T Sardona and 246T Klausenpass; K&F 12 Glarnerland
Transport	Cable car to Ampächli, Postbus (Elm–Obererbs/Matt), bus, train (Elm–Schwanden–Linthal)
Accommodation	Obererbs (3hr 15min) – Skihütte Obererbs (dormitory accommodation); Linthal – hotels, campsite

This is quite a tough day's walking, but it takes you through some charming mountain country with big views and lots of variety. There are two passes to cross. The first is an unnamed saddle in a ridge spur just below a point shown on the map as the Erbser Stock; the second is the Richetlipass, north of the Hausstock. Between the two lies the pastoral Wichlenmatt basin, which is likely to be ringing with cowbells in summer, and full of flowers before the cows are brought up to graze.

Since this is a fairly demanding stage, walkers might be tempted to ease it by taking a postbus ride to Obererbs, a saving of about 2hr 30min. The option of road-walking to Obererbs also saves about an hour, while taking the cable car to Ampächli would save around 1hr 30min of walking.

A new Berghaus just after Ampächli

Just above the church in **Elm**, turn right at Gasthaus Segnes and take an underpass, turning right and then left onto a path that climbs steeply uphill. This old mule trail rises steadily in the trees, and joins and leaves the road as it climbs towards **Ampächli** with its cable car station at 1485m, some 500m above Elm (**1hr 30min**). ◄

At one point streetlights along a road are encased in padding, presumably for mountain bikers and similar daredevils, rather than struggling walkers.

At the Ampächli restaurant complex turn south, signed to Obererbs and the Richetlipass. The higher VA path and a quicker, lower route on tracks re-join at **Hangstboden**, a group of old wooden farm buildings. After climbing, keep to the waymarked VA trail and drop into a stream-filled

Looking back from the attractive village of Elm with the Martinsloch just visible

60

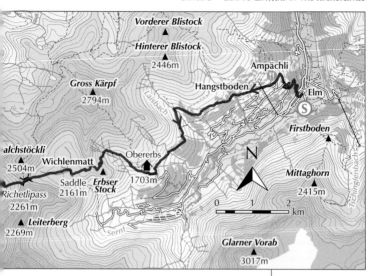

valley, contour down and into woods before climbing steadily to **Ski Hütte Obererbs** at 1703m, a lively place on a sunny weekend (**3hr 15min**).

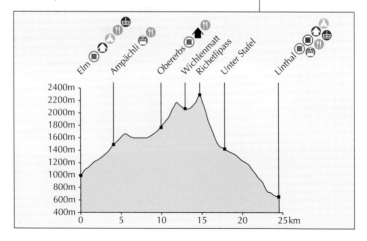

Skihütte Obererbs 28 dormitory places, open Easter–October Wednesday to Sunday. (For reservations tel 055 642 50 53, www.obererbs.ch.) The bus journey terminates here – a 20–25min ride from the station in Elm. This may be the last water for some hours, so ensure you are well supplied.

From the Ski Hütte continue on a well-marked path that will no doubt be churned by cattle. At a large rock beside the trail (1740m), a blue-and-white waymark indicates the start of a mountain route which climbs the 2794m Gross Kärpf, whose summit crowns the ridge to the north. Keep left here – the route rises at a steady gradient into a side valley and crosses several minor streams, coming to an upper pastureland bowl about half an hour from the roadhead (**3hr 45min** from Elm).

Cross the stream in the valley-head and climb southwest in a series of zigzags up a grassy spur, where you then contour round to the fine **saddle** (marked on the map as 2161m) near the Erbser Stock (**4hr 30min**). From this saddle you gain a direct view into the Wichlenmatt basin, a lovely flower-splashed grassland with the obvious saddle of the Richetlipass to the west. ◄

The descending path sweeps in long loops to the solitary alp building of **Wichlenmatt** (2037m, **4hr 45min**, possible refreshments in high summer). Bear right on a waymarked path leading into the pastures, then cross the stream to rise gently westward before tackling the final climb up steep zigzags that become even steeper just below the **Richetlipass** (2261m, **5hr 30min**). The slopes leading to the pass can be snow-covered well into the summer. If this be the case, and the path is lost, kick your way up with care and beware of cornices on the pass itself.

The Richetlipass is a narrow saddle between the Leiterberg and Chalchstöckli, and it overlooks the deep valley of the Durnachtal into which you now have to descend. A sign at the pass gives 3hr 15min to Linthal. ◄

Looking back to the north-east, much of yesterday's descent from the Foopass can be seen.

It is a long descent, coming after a long climb.

At first, the descent is very steep on a narrow twisting path that can be slippery when wet. Lower down it improves shortly before you reach a small hut on a hillside spur. Beyond this the path swings right, then drops to a moraine crest. There follows a very pleasant walk along the crest. On reaching its end you skirt the final cone along its right-hand side and descend steeply beside rough crags (and among a clutter of wild raspberries and long-stemmed gentians) to the valley bed of the Durnachtal. ▶ The continuing trail swings right and brings you to a wooden bridge crossing to the left bank of the Durnagel stream near the farm of **Unter Stafel** (1386m, **7hr**, possible summer refreshments).

Just beyond the farm a track returns you to the right bank and strikes down-valley with views ahead to Ortstock, Bös Fulen and Bächistock that wall the Linth valley. Passing the farms of Längstafel (1314m) and **Berg** (1231m) the track becomes paved.

The Richetlipass is a narrow col between two mountains with a steep upper section

One rock outcrop of several amazingly twisted strata can only be described as 'geology having a party'.

The paved road leads all the way to Linthal, but the VA takes a footpath which leaves the road at a 1177m path junction and is signed Linthal Bachweg. This cuts left to the corner of a sloping meadow, where you then turn right and follow the bottom edge of the meadow as far as a gate. Descend alongside woodland, then into the woodland itself, which is on a steep slope. The path descends in zigzags (take care if wet, as rocks on the path can be very greasy) and eventually arrives at a stream and a track where you bear right (about 15min from the road). After about 150 metres leave the track and descend on the next section of path. At first steeply down, the way becomes an old mule path making a gently sloping traverse of the wooded hillside, before zigzagging down to pass through a short tunnel blasted from the rocks. Out of this, continue for a short distance to the paved road where you wander down for 15min or so to reach Matt. Continue ahead for the station or turn left and shortly enter **Linthal** (650m, **8hr 45min**).

LINTHAL (650M)

Together with neighbouring Matt, Linthal may not have the neat compact qualities of some other villages along the route, but it's a pleasant enough place in which to spend a night. It's the highest village in the Linth valley, which is headed by the snow gemmed Tödi (3614m), the so-called 'King of the Little Mountains' and the main peak of an attractive group which was one of the earliest Alpine massifs to be explored. Linthal is the railhead of a branch line off the main Zürich–Chur railway, and the start of a postbus route across the Klausenpass to Altdorf.

Tourist information (www.glarnerland.ch and www.braunwald.ch). Hotels, restaurants, post office, bank, supermarket, railway station, buses. Accommodation: Hotel-Restaurant Adler (rooms and dormitory, tel 079 682 06 06, http://adler-linthal.business.site); Hotel Eidgenossen (closed Thursday, tel 055 643 25 28 www.restaurant-eidgenossen.business.site); Hotel Raben (closed Tuesday and Wednesday, tel 055 643 31 22, www.hotelraben.ch) and Hotel Tödi (tel 055 653 50 70, www.hoteltoedi.ch, closed Mondays).

STAGE 4
Linthal to Urnerboden by Braunwald

Start	Linthal 650mm
Finish	Urnerboden 1383m
Distance	17.5km (16km from Braunwald funicular bottom station)
Total ascent	1030m
Total descent	300m
Time	5hr 30min
High point(s)	Path after Nussbüel 1480m
Maps	LS 246T Klausenpass; K&F 12 Glarnerland
Transport	Funicular (Linthal–Braunwald); Postbus (Linthal–Urnerboden–Altdorf)
Accommodation	Braunwald (2hr) – backpackers' hostel, hotels; Urnerboden – gasthaus with dormitory accommodation

The staging to Urnerboden allows a shorter day before the long stages to Altdorf and Engelberg and after the long day to Linthal. Tactically the trek from Linthal to Altdorf can be shortened by using the postbus which covers the entire route, but Urnerboden, with its hotel and shop, makes a fine overnight stop before tackling the Klausenpass.

Starting with a climb on a well-graded path to Braunwald, an attractive resort, the way skirts the hillside past Nussbüel with great views of Tödi, at 3612m the highest peak in the region, before turning into the Urner Boden valley with ever-expanding views both up the valley and into the mountains to north and south, walking beneath the high cliffs of the Ortstock.

Make for the funicular station, which is located by the railway station in **Linthal**. From the centre of the village retrace your route to the end of Stage 3 and then head west to the station, following signs past village housing. The funicular is just after the station (**15min**).

The ascent path starts directly behind the funicular station. Turn immediately left on the signed path. From here on it's simple, up, with almost no option and almost no change in angle for a straight 600m vertical ascent.

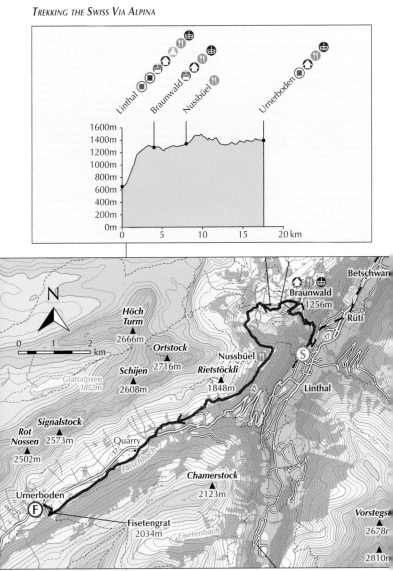

The path is superbly graded and well maintained so it's a pleasure to climb. At 1175m pass a small chapel on the right and a large rehabilitation centre on the left before meeting a road. Turn right and then right again before coming out at the top funicular station at **Braunwald** (1256m, **1hr 45min**).

The steep upper rocks of the Ortstock above Braunwald

> **Braunwald** Refreshments; accommodation includes Adrenalin Backpackers Hostel with 60 beds (tel 079 347 29 05, www.adrenalin.gl); Alexander's Tödiblick with 40 beds (tel 055 653 63 63, www.toediblick.ch); and Hüttenberg-Lodge with 31 rooms (tel 055 653 64 64, www.huetten-berg-lodge.ch). Tourist information (tel 055 653 65 65, www.braunwald.ch).

You are suddenly thrown into a place of minor hustle and bustle, with horses and carts and people milling around planning their next moves, the latter having just arrived in the village on the funicular.

It's a complicated junction, but essentially follow the road sharp left on a hairpin bend, avoiding all other distractions. There are few signs after the turn. Pass a series of ageing and not very menacing red devils signed on lampposts, and the Tödihalle where concerts are held, before passing the substantial Hüttenberg cable car station. ▶

There are big views south towards the Tödi.

The restaurant has magnificent views, and is positioned so that you are almost certain to be ready for either morning coffee or an early lunch.

Pass between chalets and descend steadily. There is a fine view ahead of the Ortstock and the Riete. The rock strata above are wildly convoluted, turned all angles by geological forces. A track joins from the left just before the path crosses a stream and a good trail continues on to **Nussbüel** (refreshments). ◄

After Nussbüel the track becomes a path and climbs through woods for 200m, gradually turning east into the valley of the Fatschbach, reaching the day's high point of 1480m. The mountains above are reminiscent of the Dolomites, while Urnerboden is in view in the flat pastoral valley below, with glacier covered Clariden above the Klausenpass also clearly seen. The path joins a road near a series of large erratic blocks and descends past farm buildings. At the third hairpin, continue ahead above the farm (Vorder Stafel), and after an attractive small farm which may sell cheese, reach a left turn through pastures down to the main valley road. ◄

Take care as the road is busy, especially with motorcyclists at weekends.

Continue up the road for 500 metres, then turn left (surprisingly) into a small **quarry** and gravel works. Bear right through the gravel heaps (!) with a sudden absence of waymarks, and continue through parking areas alongside the river where, reassuringly, the waymarks return. ◄ Press on, crossing a bridge to the south bank and later re-crossing and continuing beside the river with your destination seen ahead. The path eventually branches away from the river and climbs into the village of **Urnerboden**, sited on a moraine, whose attractive church stands guard over the valley (1383m, **5hr 30min**).

On summer weekends this area becomes an informal camp and barbecue site with families treating it as a surrogate beach.

Residents of the Urner Boden valley

The attractive hamlet of Urnerboden is dominated by its church (which also houses a small shop)

URNERBODEN (1383M)

The delightful high valley of Urner Boden, gouged out by a long-vanished glacier, is one of the finest in this part of Switzerland. On the northern flank a long ridge (the Jegerstöck) extends from the Ortstock to the Lackistock, and is almost Dolomitic in appearance, while the southern wall is dominated by Gemsfairenstock and Clariden, both of which retain small glaciers. At the foot of the Clariden lies the valley's headwall of Klus (or Chlus), down which a waterfall drains the upper glacier and snowfields. Dotted with herdsmen's huts and dairy farms, the valley bed is rich grassland interrupted by small marshy areas, providing summer grazing for around a thousand cattle (it's Switzerland's largest alp). The cantonal boundary between Glarus and Uri crosses the valley's lower end and runs along the crest of the walling ridges.

Hotel, gasthof, refreshments, post office, shop. Beds and dormitory accommodation at: Gasthof Urnerboden (tel 055 643 14 16, www.gasthaus-urnerboden.ch) and Gasthaus Sonne (tel 055 643 15 12, www.gasthaussonne.ch, reached about 2km before Urnerboden on the road. Although small, gathered around a square below the church (with shop attached), the village has an unworldly attraction, and makes an excellent base for a few days of an active holiday, for there's plenty of good walking to be had both in and along the flanks of the valley. The valley is also popular with cross-country skiers in winter. Tourist information (tel 055 643 21 31, www.urnerboden.ch).

STAGE 5
Urnerboden to Altdorf by the Klausenpass

Start	Urnerboden 1383m
Finish	Altdorf 458m
Distance	28km
Total ascent	1000m
Total descent	1920m
Time	8hr 30min
High point(s)	Klausenpass 1948m
Maps	LS 246T Klausenpass; K&F 12 Glarnerland
Transport	Postbus (Linthal–Altdorf)
Accommodation	Klausenpass (2hr 30min) – hotel with dormitory accommodation; Urigen – hotel with dormitory accommodation; Altdorf – hotels, campsite

The valley of Urner Boden bears a strong visual resemblance to parts of Norway and is loud with the clanging of cowbells as the path works its way up to the Klausenpass. Once over the pass, the Via Alpina runs high on the north side of the Schächental with spectacular views to the south, and the next day's walking to the west. After the 600m climb to the Klausenpass the walking is mainly downhill, but there are still several climbs on the long descent.

Although the path has been re-routed to avoid the road (adding around 1hr to the route), it is worth considering taking the bus from one of the higher villages such as Spiringen as far as Bürglen, Altdorf or Attinghausen, although it would be a shame to miss the details of the life of William Tell related on a series of path-side boards between Burgelen and Altdorf. For those looking to reduce the walking time on the long day to Engelberg (Stage 6), finishing Stage 5 by taking the lift to one of the berggasthauses or the refuge above Brüsti is viable, even recommended.

Options to add challenge to the day include a high-level route to the Klausenpass and a steep descent to the romantic hamlet of Äsch to take a close look at the 90m Stäubifall. Both rejoin the main route.

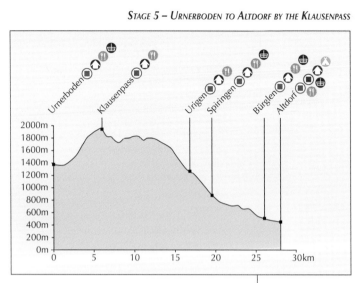

Go down to the path beside the river in **Urnerboden** and turn west (right). Continue along the riverside through pastures as the path gently climbs into woods; it meets the road after 40min. Cross the road and begin the climb proper. The path becomes wider and after climbing 150m joins the road for about 100 metres before climbing above it once more.

Looking down the long valley of the Urner Boden from the climb to the Klausenpass

One particularly long open hillside stretch provides good views back down-valley and brings you onto the road again at yet another hairpin bend (1800m), with the alp buildings of Vorfrutt seen a short distance downhill. Walk down the road as far as a stream and take a signed track on the right. This climbs in easy zigzags to high pastures well away from the road and brings you directly to the **Klausenpass** (1948m, **2hr 15min**, refreshment kiosk, public toilets, bus stop, tiny chapel). About 1.5km down the Altdorf side, accommodation (beds and dormitory places) can be had at the **Hotel Klausenpasshöhe** (tel 041 879 11 64, www.klausenpasshoehe.ch).

Though not particularly high for an Alpine pass, at 1948m the **Klausenpass** has been used for centuries to connect the cantons of Uri and Glarus, and was one of the first of the Swiss passes made accessible to motorised traffic. The pass itself is open only in summer (June to October), while the 47km-long Klausen road that crosses it between Linthal and Altdorf is scenically spectacular.

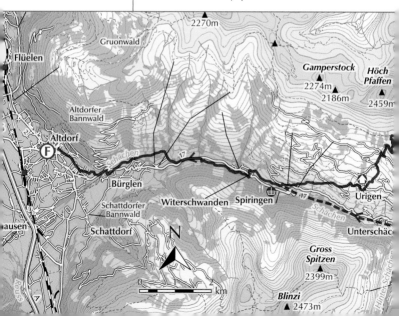

The descent begins just beyond the public toilets where a signpost indicates the path to Unter Balm and Äsch. This path runs below the road and after about 15min crosses a narrow farm track which serves the alp farm of Niemerstafel. Continue down (two paths upwards head to the Klausenpasshöhe hotel), cross a stream and reach the road (1763m) 30min after leaving the pass. ▶

The alternative route via Äsch branches off here.

For the main VA go up the road for 200 metres and take the track straight ahead. This climbs steadily amongst high farms, eventually reaching 1860m at Heidmanegg. ▶ After 15min, take the path right as it climbs sharply above the track and continue the lengthy high traverse, coming to a junction where you turn left. Descend steeply, merge into a track and then a road before a turn left down by an attractive stream. When the path meets the road, turn left though a farm and across fields, and then right more steeply downhill. The path is faint and it leads between farms and meadows, eventually coming out on the pass road at **Urigen** (1280m, **5hr 30min**).

In good weather the views across the valley and down to the Äsch waterfall are spectacular.

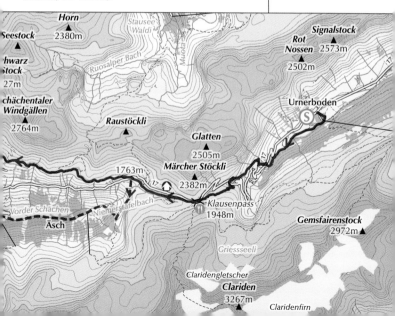

The Surenenpass and its surrounding mountains are a day's walk ahead from this section of the route after the Klausenpass

Urigen Refreshments, beds and dormitory accommodation at Hotel Posthaus (tel 041 879 11 53, www.hotel-posthaus.ch).

Wayside shrines depicting the stations of the cross accompany the path.

Continue along a track that heads diagonally down. ◄ At a (currently poorly signed) fork in the track keep left. The track continues and delivers you into the attractive village of **Spiringen** (970m, **6hr 15min**, shops, cafes, buses).

Pass through the village on the road through the square, past a school and continue on a well-built path, coming to the next village of **Witerschwanden**. Drop to the road and cross the river, then turn right. After about 2km the path re-crosses and follows the road before climbing abruptly on the north of the road. Pass under the Biel cable car and cross a bridge over the Holdenbach stream. Pass above the Brugg cable car station and continue to traverse before descending on steep wooden steps to cross the Schachen river and climb past sports facilities into **Bürglen** (553m, **8hr**).

Celebrated as the birthplace of **William Tell**, the 16th-century chapel beside the village church has been built on what is thought to be the site of Tell's house. The chapel is decorated with scenes depicting the life of this major Swiss hero, and there's a Tell Museum nearby which contains an entertaining and informative English-language slide show. Between Bürglen and Altdorf a series of boards relate Tell's life and how it fits in with the rebellion against the Hapsburg overlords.

Cross the cobbled square by the church with attractive houses and descend a cobble-stepped staircase. After crossing a river (Schächen) turn right, signed to Altdorf. The path makes its way past houses and fields and then factories and shops before emerging in the centre of **Altdorf** (458m, **8hr 30min**).

ALTDORF (458M)

Capital of canton Uri, Altdorf is inescapably 'Tell's town' with a large bronze statue by Kissling (the Telldenkmal, dated 1895) in the main square, the Rathausplatz, on the site where, according to legend, Tell had to shoot the apple from his son's head. Much of the original town was destroyed by fire in 1799, yet Altdorf retains plenty of character and some of the old pre-fire houses remain, including the 16th-century Jauch Haus used by General Suworow (see Stage 2) during his campaign against the French in 1799.

William Tell statue in Rathausplatz in Altdorf

Tourist information (tel 041 874 12 12, www.altdorf.ch). Hotels, restaurants, camping, shops, banks, post office, bus, and railway. Accommodation at: Hotel Reiser (tel 041 870 10 67), Hotel Höfli (tel 041 875 02 75, www.hotel-hoefli.ch), Hotel Goldener Schlüssel (tel 041 870 80 90, www.schluessel-altdorf.ch), Hotel Schwarzen Löwen (tel 041 874 80 80, www.hotel-loewen-altdorf.ch).

Alternative route to the Klausenpass

By taking the Fisetengrat cable car from Urnerboden, a high traverse under the Gemsfairenstock can be taken to the Klausenpass, but as this takes 3–3hr 30min it is likely that you would need to take public transport, either from the pass, Urigen or Spiringen, to reach Altdorf in good time.

Alternative descent via Äsch

From the point where the route meets the road at 1763m, turn left. The path crosses a stream a few paces from the road, but immediately before this turn left onto a minor path which leads to the farm buildings of Unter Balm (1728m, **2hr**). Pass these to your left and locate a way-marked continuing path which swings through a gap and, safeguarded with wooden handrails, descends in steep zigzags below a line of cliffs. It's an exciting descent, especially in mist with the path disappearing into the void below, and with nothing to indicate how far it will lead.

After the handrails have finished, and near the foot of the zigzags, remain alert for a small path branching below to the right. This descends quite steeply in places, with the Schächental stretching ahead, and the hamlet of Äsch soon coming into view. ◄

With pines and alpenroses, and a stream cascading down the right-hand hillside, this is a path to linger over.

Äsch (1234m) is an idyllic little hamlet set below a tremendous waterfall (the Stäubifall) that appears to explode from the hillside. After crossing the stream that flows from it, you come to a second part of the hamlet which consists of a few chalets and a tiny chapel. The whole setting is quite magical and justifies the walk to find it.

A clear track now carries the route down-valley, signed to Unterschächen. It leads through pastures and into woods, with the river running parallel with it off to the right, and eventually brings you to the Klausen road once more at Ribi. Here you break away on a path which sidles to the left to take you past more farms and through pastures before emerging at **Unterschächen** (**4–4hr 30min**).

UNTERSCHÄCHEN (999M)

With the Schächentaler Windgällen to the north, and the enchanting Brunnital to the south, headed by the Grosser Windgällen and the two Ruchen peaks, Unterschächen makes a fine, if low-key, mountaineering and mountain walking base. There's plenty to challenge and entice the outdoor enthusiast here and, just a short stroll away from the village, some splendid scenery unknown to the vast majority of visitors to Switzerland.

Tourist information (www.unterschaechen.ch). Hotels, gasthofs, restaurants, camping, shops, bank, post office, bus stop. Accommodation at Hotel Alpina with beds and dormitory places (tel 041 879 11 52, www.alpina-uri.ch), Hotel Brunnital (closed Monday, tel 041 879 11 62).

From Unterschächen to Altdorf involves either long stretches of road walking, or footpath sections within ear-shot of traffic, so it might be worth taking the postbus. There's a bus stop in the heart of the village if this is what you choose to do. For those determined to walk, how-ever, a path heads down-valley along the left bank of the river for a while before crossing and angling up to the road a short distance from the small village of **Spiringen**, where you rejoin the main route into **Altdorf**.

OPTIONS FOR SHORTENING STAGE 6

Those prepared to use public transport may find it preferable to move on to Attinghausen in readiness for crossing the Surenenpass. Cheaper accom-modation than that available in Altdorf can be found there (see panel in Stage 6 for details). If you arrived at Altdorf in good time, taking the self-service cable car to Brüsti to stay in Berggasthaus Catrina or Berghaus Brüsti would take you far from the valley bustle and give an ideal start point for the Surenenpass stage, reducing the walking time to Engelberg to a more manageable day.

STAGE 6
Altdorf to Engelberg by the Surenenpass

Start	Altdorf 458m
Finish	Engelberg 1000m
Distance	29.5km
Total ascent	2040m
Total descent	1500m
Time	10hr 30min
High point(s)	Surenenpass 2292m
Maps	LS 246T Klausenpass and 245T Stans; K&F 11 Vierwaldstättersee
Transport	Bus (Altdorf–Attinghausen); cable car (Attinghausen–Brüsti)
Accommodation	Attinghausen (45min) – hotels, with dormitory accommodation; Brüsti (3r 45min) – gasthof with dormitory accommodation; Alp Grät (4hr 30min) – mountain hut with dormitory accommodation; Blackenalp (7hr 30min) – mountain hut with dormitory accommodation; Stäfeli (8hr 30min) – berggasthaus with dormitory accommodation and simple rooms; Engelberg – hotels, gasthofs, youth hostel, camping

Although this is another exceptionally long stage, it is also one of the finest of the whole trek. The trail is clearly defined and given good weather there will be magnificent views almost every step of the way. But unless you have sufficient days in hand to turn it into a two-stage route, all but the most determined of walkers are advised to take advantage of the transport options available. You can reduce the day's demands by about 3hr, thus enabling you to enjoy it without pressure. This is, after all, a stage to absorb in every detail, and if there's a section which can be omitted it's the road walk from Altdorf to Attinghausen, and subsequent steep, mostly forested, uphill path to Brüsti. These can by relieved by taking the local bus to Attinghausen, and cable car from there.

Above Brüsti, where the cable car terminates, the approach to the Surenenpass is full of variety, and with views down to a branch of the Vierwaldstättersee (Lake Lucerne), or south into the secretive Waldnacht valley, while from the pass itself the ice-crowned Titlis is seen to the southwest. For much of the descent to Engelberg you will have that mountain in your sights.

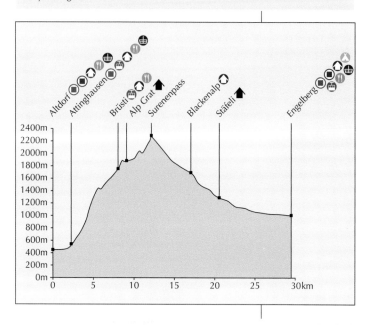

PUBLIC TRANSPORT FROM ALTDORF

Walkers intending to catch the bus from Altdorf to Attinghausen will find the bus stop near the Tell statue in the main square. Ask for Attinghausen Seilbahn. Once there you will find that the cable car station is unmanned. Using the telephone provided, alert the operator at the middle station (it's a two-stage lift) that you wish to ride the cable car. When you get a response, ask for 'Bergfahrt, bitte', enter the cable car and close the door. This signals that you're ready to start. Payment is made at the middle station.

If starting at the train station, a sign to Brüsti Seilbahn sends you to Gasthaus Walter Fürst, where you pass under the railway and join the waymarked route to Attinghausen (20min).

Start with your back to the multi-coloured theatre and information centre in **Altdorf**'s central square. ◄ Follow the signed VA route and then the *Wanderweg* markers heading south and then south-west from the town centre, first on a road, then on a path between houses, and then past fields and across an area of open land. On reaching a main road, go under the railway line then the motorway, and cross the River Reuss into **Attinghausen** (490m, **45min**).

ATTINGHAUSEN (490M)

The village of Attinghausen is overshadowed by its neighbour, Altdorf, but earns a place in Swiss history as the birthplace of Walter Fürst, who was one of the original conspirators against Habsburg rule. Today it appears to be something of a commuter village without much character, but it's well placed for trekkers on the VA and provides a useful alternative overnight stop to the busier and more expensive Altdorf.

Tourist information (www.attinghausen-tourismus.ch). Hotel, shop, restaurant, post office, bank, cable car to Brüsti. Accommodation at: Hotel-Restaurant Krone (beds and dormitory, tel 041 870 10 55, www.kronehotel.ch).

The path to Brüsti begins by the side of the cable car station and rises along the right-hand side of a stream, crossing near the intermediate station (**25min**) where a sign suggests it will take another 2hr 30min to reach Brüsti. The way resumes on a track that winds steeply through pasture and forest to Hochiberg, reached about 30min before coming to **Brüsti** (1528m, **3hr 45min**).

> **Brüsti** Accommodation at Berggasthaus Alp Catrina (beds and dormitory places, tel 041 871 06 38, www.brüsti-surenenpass.ch/alp-catrina) and Berggasthaus Brüsti (dormitory accommodation, tel 041 771 00 11, en.berggasthaus-brusti.com).

Outside the cable car station a signpost indicates the uphill path to the Surenenpass. It takes you past a few houses (including Berghaus Alp Catrina (formerly

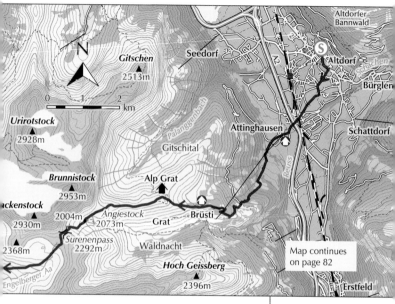

Z'Graggen)), and along a short, vegetated crest bright with alpenroses in early summer, and with bilberries and stunted pine trees. A short rail-guarded section descends a little, with views down into a scoop of pasture with a few farms and huts below, and across Altdorf's valley to mountains flanking the Schächental.

Passing the mountain hut at Alp Grat with early morning cloud rising from the valley

At **Alp Grat** (1820m, **4hr 30min**, refreshments and dormitory accommodation; mob 078 745 95 57, tel 041 870 19 60, www.alp-grat-surenenpass.ch) 45min from Brüsti, there's a path junction. For the Surenenpass the way angles up and across the hillside to a grassy crest from which you gain a first sighting of the Urnersee leg of the Vierwaldstättersee.

AN EVER-CHANGING LANDSCAPE

The first time I walked this route views were clear and unhindered off to the lake and far away to Switzerland's eastern ranges, while wisps of mist played among the grey crags ahead. But the next time all this was reversed as a huge cloud-sea hid all sign of lake and valley, while the ridges of Brunnistock and Blackenstock were sharp in the morning light, their crests outlined with brushstrokes of cornice. Both occasions were full of magic.

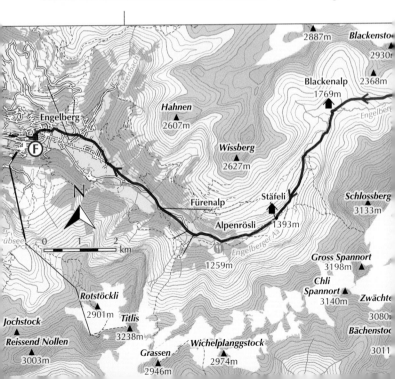

Beyond Grat's green crest you come to a signpost in a saddle (2060m) under the **Angiestock** (2073m, **5hr 15min**). Directly ahead you can see the pass (signed as 1hr away) across a long slope of scree. The path now loses a little height over a rocky area to a path junction, Langschnee (2004m), where one path descends left into the lovely Waldnacht valley, while ours continues ahead over more rocks and, often as the name implies, snowfields, before steepening with zigzags to gain the **Surenenpass** (2292m), about 6hr 15min from Altdorf, or 2hr 30min from Brüsti.

The pass is a rewarding place (given settled weather, that is), for it offers a wonderful vista dominated by the 3238m Titlis which grabs your attention from the south-west, yet seems so far-off as to make it difficult to believe that tomorrow's route crosses its shoulder. Below the pass lie the Seewen tarns, trapped in rucks of pasture. ▸

The descent route from the pass curves left, passes an emergency shelter and for an hour or so swings down through pastures grazed by sheep, before becoming a track that leads to **Blackenalp** (1769m, **7hr 15min**).

Looking ahead from the Angiestock saddle. The path crosses the bottom of the scree on a good trail

Although the path does not visit them, they make a perfect picnic site, and it's easy to rejoin the onward route, should you decide to visit their shores.

Alphütte Blackenalp Accommodation (dormitory places), refreshments (tel 041 637 04 26). A very fine backdrop of a steep-walled mountain cirque topped by the 2887m Wissigstock and Blackenstock (2930m).

Nearby stands an attractive little white walled chapel; the path passes this, goes through a natural 'gateway' and crosses the Stierenbach on a stone bridge to break into an open section of valley. In another 20min it recrosses to the right bank of the stream and comes to a junction. Take the left fork after the bridge near a waterfall and continue down to **Stäfeli** (1393m, **8hr 15min**).

Berggasthaus Stäfeli Accommodation, refreshments, open late May–late October (tel 041 637 45 11, www.staefeli.ch).

From the terrace of the Berggasthaus, your attention is inevitably drawn across the valley to a series of cascades, and the stab of aiguilles of the **Spannort peaks** rising against the skyline.

Beyond Stäfeli the track sidles downhill for another 20–30min to **Restaurant Alpenrösli** (1259m, refreshments) where a path breaks off to the left and crosses the Stierenbach. The path now takes you over pastures and through woods below Titlis, until you are drawn back across the river and onto the track leading to a paved road. This brings you to the **Fürenalp** cable car station and, soon after, the Wasserfall restaurant. Pass the golf course and take a path that forks right off the road. This path, which merges into quiet roads, carries you all the way to Engleberg, coming into the town above the monastery. Turn left down steps before the large school, then right at the bottom of a staircase and in 2hr 15min from Stäfeli, 7hr from Brüsti and 10hr 30min from Altdorf, enter the centre of **Engelberg** (1000m).

Approaching Engelberg the many walking opportunities in the region become apparent

ENGELBERG (1000M)

The first of the major mountain resorts visited along the VA, Engelberg makes an excellent walking centre with a number of good routes, several of which are aided by a variety of cableways. The town is much older than tourism, for it developed around a huge Benedictine monastery founded in 1120, but was rebuilt following a fire in the 18th century. The monastery, or abbey, was named by Pope Calixtus II, Mons Angelorum (from whose German form the present-day Engelberg is derived). Its main attraction for mountain tourists is, of course, the Titlis, while climbers turn to the Spannörter which flank the valley further upstream.

Tourist information (tel 041 639 77 77, www.engelberg.ch). Hotels, youth hostel, campsite, restaurants, shops, banks, post office, bus services, trains to Lucerne, cable cars. Of the many hotel options, lower-priced accommodation includes Pension St Jakob (dormitory options, tel 041 637 45 35, www.st-jakobpension.ch), Spannort Inn (dormitory options, tel 041 511 11 10, alpapartments.ch/en), Hotel Bellevue-Terminus (tel 041 639 68 68, www.bellevue-terminus.ch). The youth hostel (112 dormitory beds, tel 041 637 12 92, www.youthhostel.ch/engelberg) is located on the way to the Trübsee gondola lift. The campsite, Camping Eienwäldli (tel 041 637 19 49, www.eienwaeldli.ch) has excellent facilities, including indoor swimming pool and on-site shop – open all year except November.

STAGE 7
Engelberg to Engstlenalp by the Jochpass

Start	Engelberg 1000m
Finish	Engstlenalp 1835m
Distance	12km
Total ascent	1280m
Total descent	450m
Time	5hr
High point(s)	Jochpass 2208m
Maps	LS 245T Stans and 255T Sustenpass; K&F 11 Vierwaldstättersee
Transport	Gondola lift (Engelberg–Trübsee); chairlift (Trübsee–Jochpass); chairlift (Jochpass–Engstlenalp); postbus (Engstlenalp–Meiringen)
Accommodation	Trübsee (2hr 30min) – hotel; Jochpass (4hr) – berghaus with dormitory accommodation; Engstlenalp – hotel with dormitory accommodation

This stage could be merged with the following one to Meiringen which, if walked in its entirety, would make another very long and demanding day. But there are plenty of cable car options available, so it's perfectly feasible to reduce the actual walking time to suit your own needs.

However, the walk to Engstlenalp covers interesting ground and if you are looking for a shorter day there is plenty to see, although the scenic delights are spoilt somewhat by the number of lifts around the Trübsee and Jochpass. It would also allow a longer-than-usual lunch in one of the mountain restaurants, or even a side trip by cable car to the summit of Titlis, while the descent to Engstlenalp has the sparkle of the Engstlensee to entice you downhill.

Facing away from **Engelberg** railway station, turn left and follow signs that direct you past houses and across fields to cross to the south of the river to Hotel Bänklialp. Here turn up through forest, climbing steeply in places to reach the open meadowland of Vorder Stafel (1256m),

where refreshments can be had at **Restaurant Gerschnialp** about 50min from Engelberg.

The way now heads towards the steepening slope past ski-tows, then up a long series of zigzags while silver gondolas swing overhead with effortless ease. The path becomes even steeper towards the top of this section, before you emerge with relief to a sudden levelling by the side of the gondola lift station and the **Trübsee** (1788m, **2hr 30min**).

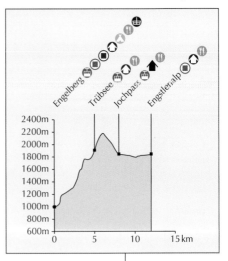

Berghotel Trübsee Accommodation, refreshments, (tel 041 639 50 92, www.hoteltruebsee.ch).

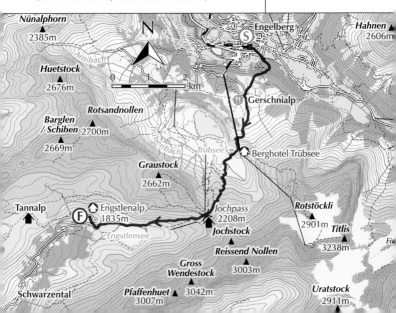

Boating on the Trübsee

TITLIS

Despite its lacework of cableways, Titlis is a fine-looking mountain of 3238m. It was the first snow mountain in Switzerland to be climbed, the ascent being made in 1739 by Ignaz Herz, JE Waser and two other Engelberg men, but nowadays you can take the world's first revolving gondola to the Klein Titlis (3029m) along the ridge west of the main summit (a 45min climb), and find the highest karaoke bar in Europe – as well as the ubiquitous souvenir stands and ice grotto. Summit views are extensive, stretching across much of the Alpine chain from the snows of Mont Blanc to the Tyrol. Germany's Black Forest and the Jura crest which carries the Franco–Swiss border can also be seen, but it is the big peaks of the Oberland that provide the main focus of attention.

Wander ahead down a track into a large plateau dominated by the Trübsee. Soaring above the plateau is the Titlis, its tilted glacier appealing to skiers year-round.

Walk round the left-hand end of the lake towards the Jochpass chairlift. After crossing a bridge, turn left and soon begin the climb which then takes about a further hour to reach the **Jochpass** (2208m, **4hr**).

> **Jochpass** Accommodation (26 beds, dormitory places), refreshments at Berghaus Jochpass, open June–end September (tel 041 637 11 87, www. jochpass.ch).

Perhaps the least satisfying of all the crossings on the VA, the Jochpass nevertheless is easy to escape from. Simply take the continuing path that descends south-west beneath yet another chairlift. Fortunately, you soon lose this on the way down to the Engstlensee, a large oval lake seen some 300m below. There's another lake in view too, the Tannensee, lying in a high valley west of the Engstlensee passed in the next stage. ▶

Looking back to the Trübsee from the Jochpass climb on a wintry day in September

Ahead the Wetterhorn appears like a giant meringue-topped cake, a vision that remains with you for several hours.

89

A warm welcome awaits at the Hotel Engstlenalp

The **Engstlensee** (1850m, **4hr 30min**) lies within a sweep of pasture, its south bank rising steeply to the peaks and hanging glaciers of the Wendestick, which extends a ridge running from the Titlis. The lakeside is understandably popular with picnic parties and anglers, for a road (served by postbus) approaches within a few hundred metres, so access is straightforward. A track draws away from the lakeside and leads directly to **Engstlenalp** (1835m, **5hr**).

ENGSTLENALP (1835M)

Considered in 1866 by Professor John Tyndall, vice-president of the Alpine Club, to be 'one of the most charming spots in the Alps', Engstlenalp consists of a broad open pasture at the head of the lovely Gental. The alp is dotted with farm buildings, and a section of it is designated as a nature reserve. A number of walks radiate from it, and the Victorian hotel makes an atmospheric base for a few days' walking holiday.

Accommodation, refreshments at Hotel Engstlenalp, open May–end October, 60 beds, 60 dormitory places (tel 033 975 11 61, www.engstlenalp.ch).

STAGE 8
Engstlenalp to Meiringen by Planplatten

Start	Engstlenalp 1035m
Finish	Meiringen 595m
Distance	22.5km
Total ascent	730m
Total descent	1960m
Time	7hr
High point(s)	Balmeregghorn 2255m
Maps	LS 245T Stans and 255T Sustenpass; K&F 19 Gotthard
Transport	Postbus (Engstlenalp–Meiringen); cable car (Planplatten–Reuti–Meiringen)
Accommodation	Hasliberg Reuti (5–5hr 30min) – hotels, gasthofs and dormitory accommodation; Schwarzental (alternative route 1hr) – beds and dormitory accommodation; Meiringen – hotels, gasthofs, camping, dormitory accommodation

Today has one of the highlights of the VA, the Erzegg/Planplatten ridge. This traverses high above the Gental, with views in all directions and ahead to the giants of the Bernese Oberland. This splendid ridge is airy but not exposed and experienced trekkers will relish the walk. But in poor weather, particularly high winds or storms (or the risk of storm), it would be best avoided and lower alternative routes described below (which are also fine walks) should be taken instead.

Along the traverse, views are of Sustenhorn, Dammastock and other peaks of the Urner Oberland; from Planplatten onwards the eye will be drawn to Grosse Scheidegg, the Wetterhorn and the high mountains of the Bernese Oberland above Grindelwald. On a clear day, make sure your camera battery is fully charged and its memory has plenty of space, but be aware that you won't have the route to yourself, for the Planplatten cable car makes it a great day-walk as well. Use of this cableway is a tempting option, especially for trekkers combining this stage with the previous one from Engelberg, for it cuts out a long, 1600m descent to Meiringen – downhill almost all the way.

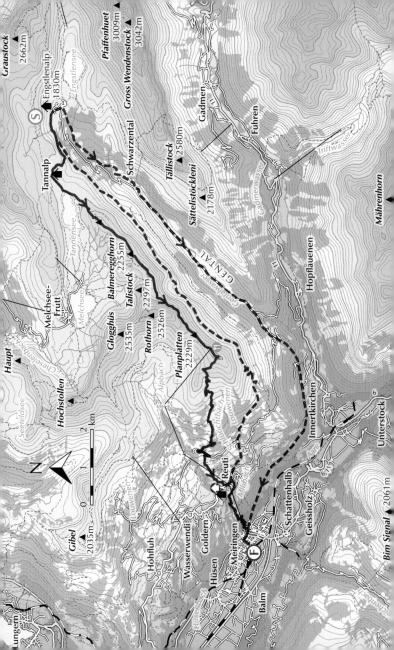

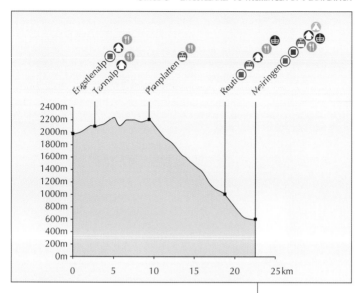

From **Hotel Engstlenalp** take the path heading to the right, signed to Hasliberg and Melchsee, which takes you past haybarns and farms with fine views both up- and down-valley, then swings westward over a stream. When the path forks, take the upper branch leading to the Tannensee and the small resort of Melchsee-Frutt. ▶

The left (lower) fork is an alternative route to Reuti (see below).

Snow over the Oberland mountains, looking from Engstlenalp

Making a rising traverse below cliffs walling the valley, the path brings you onto a grassy crest (Berggastghaus Tannalp accommodation and refreshments, tel 041 669 12 41, www.tannalp.ch) over which you descend to the **Tannensee (1hr)**. Take the track along the east shore, then a path which climbs south-west across the slopes of Erzegg to the cross that marks the summit at 2140m. Continue in the same direction on a good path along the ridge, mainly on the narrow crest but sometimes just below it. ◄

It is an airy route, but with little exposure and with magnificent views all the way.

After 2hr drop to a small saddle where there is a path running below the ridge that would provide a safe exit in the event of a storm. At another dip in the ridge a blue Alpine path that starts a short distance to the right could be taken if time allowed for a 2–3hr ascent of the Talistock and Rothorn, making an interesting diversion for those who are prepared for airy ridge scrambling.

Approaching the Balmeregghorn, the highest part of the Erzegg ridge. This shows the steepest part; the exposure is modest

The route goes over the **Balmeregghorn** (2255m), more a high point on the ridge than a peak, then follows a rocky moraine rib to a saddle, looking down over a fine hanging valley one way, with a long drop to the Gental on the other. It then makes a splendid high traverse, with ever-improving views into the Bernese Alps, high up on the mountainside (but below the actual crest), and leads

Looking down to the village of Reuti, where there is a cable car to Meiringen if required

to **Planplatten** (2229m, **3hr 30min**, refreshments, cable car). From there you have a choice of routes: footpath to Gummenalp, Reuti and Meiringen, or take the 'Eagle-Express' gondola to Mägisalp, Reuti and Meiringen.

The walking route continues after the Planpatten station and turns right 10min further along the ridge. Windsocks are suggestive of hang-gliding. The long descent starts steadily through high pasture. ▶

After 30min reach a small farm, then a track. Continue down, taking a left fork in the track and passing through the farm of Gummenalp, then another alp where a path leads you past a dairy (possible refreshments). After a short stretch of road towards woods, the path's gradient steepens and descends over rooted slopes. Turn right at a road and then left on a well-made track that features Hasli, a local cartoon character, on a series of boards. This track meets and crosses the road twice. At a staircase whose apparent function is merely to cut off a small bend, take the path downhill through fields. It becomes a track and descends into **Reuti** (1065m, **6hr**) close to the Hasliberg cable car station, where the descending path is indicated on the left.

The views change here, looking directly across to the Grosse Scheidegg with the Wetterhorn and Eiger showing fine profiles, with hints of what lies behind.

95

HASLIBERG–REUTI (1065M)

This is a small village resort set high above the Haslital. Linked by cable car with Meiringen, another extends to Bidmi and from there to Mägisalp. From Mägisalp a gondola lift continues to Planplatten at 2245m, thereby giving access to some of the fine walking country enjoyed on the trek from Engstlenalp described above.

Refreshments, accommodation includes Hotel Reuti (tel 033 972 53 00, www. hotelreuti.ch), Hotel Panorama (tel 033 972 50 11, www.panorama-hasliberg.ch).

The way down to Meiringen, which takes less than an hour from here, is well signed on a reasonably graded track, starting 50 metres down from the Reuti cable car station. At the end of a long day, if time is pressing or knees or feet cry out for a rest, the cable car is a tempting option. Passing a small sculpture park halfway down, the route is signed and remains mostly in forest. Emerging near the valley cable car station, the way turns right to pass a church and the Hasli museum before turning into the centre of **Meiringen** (600m, **7hr**).

MEIRINGEN (600M)

This busy little town, situated between the River Aare and the slopes of the Hasliberg, grew in importance as a result of traffic using the Brunig, Susten and Grimsel passes. It has a long history, but few of its buildings survived two disastrous fires of 1879 and 1891. One that did is the lovely old parish church seen as you enter the town from Reuti. It has a detached Romanesque tower with a wooden spire, 14th-century frescoes inside, and 15th-century paintings of St Peter and St Michael. Meiringen claims to have seen the creation of meringue, but its most obvious claim to fame is via the death of Sherlock Holmes at the Reichenbach Falls. The Falls are one of the town's greatest tourist attractions, and Meiringen shamelessly exploits the Holmes connection with a Sherlock Holmes Museum on Conan Doyle Place. On 4 May each year members of the Sherlock Holmes Society make a visit to the Falls to commemorate the death of their fictitious hero.

Tourist information (tel 033 972 50 50, www.haslital.swiss). Many hotels, gasthofs, camping, restaurants, shops, banks, post office, postbus to Grindelwald, railway connections with Interlaken and Lucerne. Lower-priced accommodation

includes Simons Herberge (beds and dormitories, tel 033 971 17 15, www.simons-herberge.ch), in Willigen Hotel Tourist (tel 033 971 10 44, www.hotel-tourist.ch). The nearest campsite is 2km west of Meiringen across the river: Camping Balmweid (tel 033 971 51 15, www.camping-meiringen.ch).

Bad-weather alternatives
There are two lower options, as well as buses from near Hotel Engstlenalp:

Engstlenalp to Reuti via the traversing path (15km, **4hr**). This route stays below the Planplatten ridge, traversing and gently declining. If there is snow or high wind on the ridge it is recommended. Start as for Tannalp/Tannensee and after 10min take the left fork. Follow the path as it traverses 500m below the ridge above, usually well below any weather problems. Pass small farms and eventually the path becomes a track. Turn the corner towards Reuti and follow tracks, farm lanes and paths into Reuti. From **Reuti**, either follow the main descent route to **Meiringen** or take the cable car down.

Engstlenalp to Meiringen via the Gental (17km, **4hr 30min**). This is the route to take if the weather is so bad that the main or first alternative route become impractical or inadvisable. It has some very attractive features as well as transport options.

Head downhill from the Hotel Engstlenalp on Route 40. At first the path steers well clear of the road but lower down joins with it at **Schwarzental** (1369m, **1hr**, Schwarzental Refreshments at Restaurant Schwarzental. Bus stop nearby).

Continue down the road for a further hour to Alp Gental where there is another bus stop and it may be possible to visit the cheesemakers. Continue downhill and turn left off the road. At about 1050m, either continue on Route 40 to **Innertkirchen** and bus to Meiringen, or turn right and follow easy paths and tracks into **Meiringen** above the Aare river.

STAGE 9
Meiringen to Grindelwald by Grosse Scheidegg

Start	Meiringen 600m
Finish	Grindelwald 1040m
Distance	23km
Total ascent	1500m
Total descent	1060m
Time	8hr
High point(s)	Grosse Scheidegg 1962m
Maps	LS 5004 Berner Oberland; K&F 18 Jungfrau Region
Transport	Reichenbachbahn to the top of the falls near Zwirgi; bus (Meiringen–Grindelwald via Grosse Scheidegg)
Accommodation	Willigen (20min) – hotel; Zwirgi (1hr) – gasthaus; Kaltenbrunnen (1hr 45min) – gasthof with dormitory accommodation; Rosenlaui (2hr 30min) – hotel with dormitory accommodation; Schwarzwaldalp (3hr 20min) – hotel-chalet with dormitory accommodation; Grosse Scheidegg (5hr) – mountain inn with dormitory accommodation; First (alternative route 7hr) – berggasthaus with dormitory accommodation; Grindelwald – hotels, gasthofs, youth hostel, camping

Despite its length, this is a comparatively easy and straightforward stage which leads into one of the best-known regions of the Bernese Oberland, on the way passing below the steep walls of the Wetterhorn and gaining a first close view of the Eiger. Although Grindelwald is given as the destination, an alternative route is offered from Grosse Scheidegg, providing an opportunity to enjoy a high belvedere with stunning views and an overnight spent in relative peace away from Grindelwald's crowds. On the main route, an overnight at Hotel Wetterhorn would also escape the crowds, adding an hour to the following day's walk and perhaps dovetailing with an overnight in Wengen.

There are lots of refreshment opportunities along the route, and should you consider the distance more than you wish to walk – or the weather is unpromising – you can take a bus for some, or all, of the way. In Meiringen an hourly postbus leaves from the railway station, while buses to Grindelwald meet them at Schwarzwaldalp.

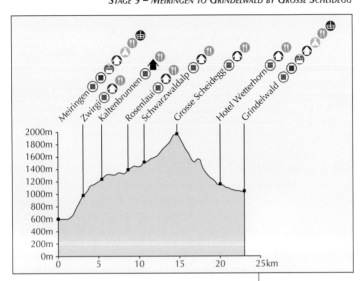

Leaving **Meiringen**, follow the main road heading south-east (direction Innertkirchen and Grimsel Pass), cross the River Aare and enter the village of **Willigen** (621m, **20min**).

Sherlock Holmes in contemplative mood before his showdown with Moriarty

Willigen Shop, refreshments, accommodation at Hotel Tourist (tel 033 971 10 44). The Reichenbachbahn starts here, going to the top of the falls some 400m above.

About 50 metres beyond Hotel Tourist, turn right along a narrow road between a house and a barn. After passing several more houses the road ends and a grass path then rises ahead, leading to another minor road which you cross to the continuing waymarked path.

This leapfrogs the road a few times, and brings you to Schwendi (792m, **40min**).

Continue along the road for a short distance, until a footpath breaks away to the right, enters forest and becomes an old, paved mule track. It passes a spectacular viewpoint for the Reichenbach Falls (845m, **1hr**), and a memorial at the spot where Holmes took Moriarty to their mutual doom. The way climbs again, crosses the road and comes to **Zwirgi**. (976m, **1hr 30min**).

> **Gasthaus Zwirgi** Bedrooms, restaurant (tel 033 971 14 22, www.zwirgi.ch).

A sign directs the way to Kaltenbrunnen in 45min. The path to take leaves the road on the left and heads through forest and meadow before rejoining the road again near **Kaltenbrunnen** (1210m, **2hr 15min**).

> **Berggasthof Kaltenbrunnen** Bedrooms, dormitory accommodation, restaurant (tel 033 971 19 08).

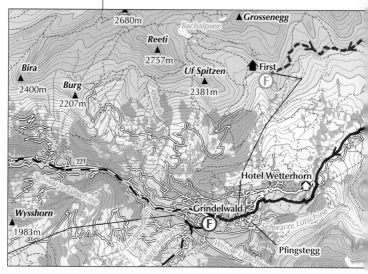

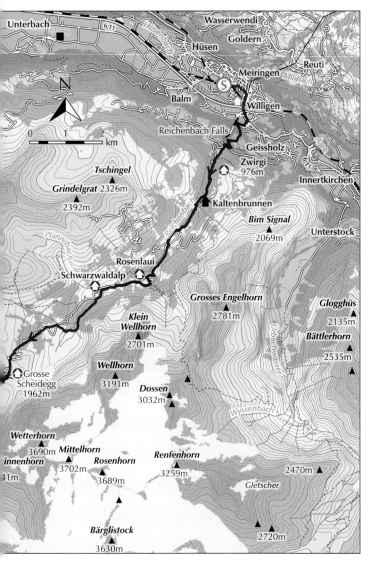

Unterbach

6;11

Wasserwendi

Hüsen

Goldern

Meiringen

Reuti

Millibach

Balm

Willigen

N

0   1   2 km

Reichenbach Falls

Geissholz

Zwirgi
976m

Innertkirchen

Tschingel

Grindelgrat 2326m

2392m

Kaltenbrunnen

Bim Signal

2069m

Unterstock

Pfannibach

Reichenbach

Rosenlaui

Schwarzwaldalp

Grosses Engelhorn

2781m

Glogghüs

2135m

Urbachwasser

Bättlerhorn

2535m

Klein Wellhorn

2701m

Wellhorn

3191m

Dossen

3032m

Wyssenbach

Grosse Scheidegg
1962m

Wetterhorn

3690m

innenhorn

Mittelhorn

3702m

Rosenhorn

3689m

Renfenhorn

3259m

2470m

Gletscher

1m

Bärglistock

3630m

2720m

101

The Reichenbach Falls

By now the gradient has eased with the valley stretching ahead, densely wooded and steep walled. Continue along the road until it makes a left-hand hairpin, at which point keep ahead on a footpath that accompanies the Reichenbach stream and, with only a brief section of road walking, takes you upvalley as far as Schwarzwaldalp. On the way it passes the farming community of Gschwantenmad (1304m, **2hr 45min**) with views of the Engelhörner peaks, the remains of the snout of the Rosenlaui glacier, and the Wetterhorn.

THE WETTERHORN

Dominating the upper valley of Grindelwald, the Wetterhorn (the fabled 'Peak of Tempests') is one of the most celebrated and easily recognised mountains in all the Alps, although it is by no means one of the highest. There are three main peaks: the Rosenhorn (3689m), Mittelhorn (3702m) and the true Wetterhorn, the Hasli Jungfrau (3690m), first climbed in August 1844 by Bannholzer and Jaun. Alfred Wills' ascent in 1854, which was so vividly described in his classic *Wanderings among the High Alps*, has been taken as the start of the so-called Golden Age of Mountaineering.

Rising at the head of the valley, keep on the left of the stream for another 15min or so to reach **Rosenlaui** (1328m, **3hr**).

Hotel Rosenlaui Massive Victorian hotel with dormitories (tel 033 971 29 12, www.rosenlaui.ch).

From the hotel a path takes you left towards the entrance to the Rosenlaui glacier gorge, then swings to the right above the road. Shortly before reaching Schwarzwaldalp the way crosses a bridge and enters the alp. A short way before you re-cross the stream stands the **Chalet-Hotel Schwarzwaldalp** (1454m, **3hr 45min**).

Chalet-Hotel Schwarzwaldalp Rooms and dormitory accommodation (tel 033 971 35 15, www.schwarzwaldalp.ch).

Chalet near Schwarzwaldalp with the Engelhörner ridge above

Return to the left side of the stream and continue upvalley among trees and shrubs, then over rough pastures before recrossing to the north side. Here you cut up the slope ahead beside the road, crossing it several times on the way to the **Grosse Scheidegg** (1962m, **5hr 30min**) where a new vista opens up.

Grosse Scheidegg Bus stop, large berghotel and restaurant with dormitory accommodation (tel 079 922 93 14, www.grosse-scheidegg.ch).

Being 99m lower than the Kleine Scheidegg (crossed on Stage 10), which limits the western side of Grindelwald's pastoral basin, the 'Grosse' (or Great) epithet of **Grosse Scheidegg** refers to the extent of the pass, rather than its height. This wide saddle dividing the Rosenlaui and Grindelwald valleys is formed by an easy ridge linking the dramatic precipices of the Wetterhorn with the modest Schwarzhorn. From the pass the view south-westward shows the tremendous wall of the Bernese Oberland, gaining a view of the Eiger in profile above sweeping meadows.

The walk to Grosse Scheidegg passes under the 3000m Wellhorn

▶ The descent from **Grosse Scheidegg** to Grindelwald begins a few paces down the road below the hotel. The signed path drops steeply at first, crosses the twisting road several times, and is waymarked all the way. It leads among shrubs and open pasture, and 1hr 30min from the pass brings you to **Hotel Wetterhorn** (1229m, **7hr**) and a large parking area for visitors to the gorge of the Upper Grindelwald glacier. Buses to Grindelwald are available here as elsewhere on the descent from Grosse Scheidegg.

The alternative route to First leaves the main route at this point.

Hotel Wetterhorn Beds and dormitory places (tel 033 853 12 18, www.wetterhorn-hotel.ch).

The signed route from here starts at the far corner of the large car park. Look for a right turn and continue through woods, meadows and then small lanes in about 1hr, to **Grindelwald** (1040m, **8hr**), an attractive finish to the day.

GRINDELWALD (1040M)

Formerly known as the 'glacier village', Grindelwald has become one of Switzerland's busiest and best-known resorts and mountaineering centres, alive and thriving equally in winter as in summer. Though shrinking fast now, its glaciers were subjected to much scientific interest in the 18th century, and 100 years later attracted the attention of inquisitive tourists. Seeing how distant from Grindelwald these glacial remnants are today, it's hard to believe that in 1723 Sir Horace Mann reported that an exorcist had been employed to halt the advance of the ice which was threatening to obliterate the village. Many of today's visitors are more attracted to the famous Jungfraujoch. Gondolas on a new lift system rise to Eigergletscher station, meeting the railway, which rises to Kleine Scheidegg, then tunnels through the Eiger to emerge at the Joch (or saddle) below the Jungfrau at an altitude of 3454m. It's the highest railway in Europe – and probably the most expensive.

Other Grindelwald attractions include the exceptional scenery and very fine walking prospects. A walking holiday based here would provide sufficient variety and stimulating exercise to last the whole summer, while for trekkers tackling the VA it makes an obvious choice for a spell of rest and recuperation before moving on.

Tourist information (tel 033 854 12 12, www.grindelwald.ch). Hotels, gasthofs, youth hostel, campsites, restaurants, shops, banks, post office, railway connections to destinations including Interlaken, Kleine Scheidegg, Wengen and Lauterbrunnen, cable car to Eigergletscher and Jungfraujoch. Many hotels in Grindelwald, with some lower-priced accommodation: youth hostel (130 dormitory places, tel 033 853 10 09, www.youthhostel.ch/grindelwald), Eiger Lodge (140 places in beds and dormitories, tel 033 854 38 38, www.eigerlodge.ch), Downtown Lodge (independent hostel with100+ beds and dormitory places, tel 033 828 77 30, downtown-lodge@jungfrau.ch), Berggasthaus Marmorbruch (mob 079 310 30 89, www.marmorbruch.ch).

Alternative route: Grosse Scheidegg to First (1hr 30min)
A splendid alternative to the standard VA descent to Grindelwald, this balcony path provides magnificent high mountain views, and leads to a restaurant with dormitory accommodation at the First gondola station. An overnight spent there gives a chance to watch sunset and sunrise over the Alps, and a recommended early morning visit to the Bachalpsee (Bachsee) for one of the truly great Alpine views. Note that if you plan to stay overnight, it is essential to phone to make a booking in advance – see details below.

Cross the road at **Grosse Scheidegg** and turn right along a track signed to First, Faulhorn and Höhenweg 2400. When the track forks, veer left, but take the footpath here, not the track. The path is the Höhenweg 2400 trail, which leads across high pastures and reaches **First** (2167m, **6hr**) about 1hr 30min from Grosse Scheidegg.

The Bachalpsee above Grindelwald, with Schreckhorn and Finsteraarhorn as a backdrop (Photo: Kev Reynolds)

> **Berggasthaus First** Dormitory places for 90, and full meals provision – booking essential (tel 033 828 77 88, www.berggasthausfirst.ch).

To visit the Bachalpsee (optional) take the broad signed path which rises above the gondola station, and in 50min reaches the lake. For the best views go to the far end and look back to the south-east. An early morning visit is highly recommended.

To rejoin the VA route, either ride the gondola down to **Grindelwald** and continue on Stage 10, or retrace your steps along the Höhenweg 2400 trail to **Grosse Scheidegg**, where you then follow directions given below for the descending path to Grindelwald.

STAGE 10

Grindelwald to Lauterbrunnen by Kleine Scheidegg

Start	Grindelwald 1040m
Finish	Lauterbrunnen 800m
Distance	19.5km
Total ascent	1150m
Total descent	1390m
Time	6hr 30min
High point(s)	Kleine Scheidegg 2061m
Maps	LS 5004 Berner Oberland; K&F 18 Jungfrau Region
Transport	Train (Grindelwald–Kleine Scheidegg–Lauterbrunnen); gondola lift (Grindelwald–Männlichen); cable car (Männlichen–Wengen)
Accommodation	Alpiglen (2hr 15min) – berghotel with dormitory accommodation; Kleine Scheidegg (3hr 45min) – hotels and dormitory accommodation; Wengen (5hr 30min) – hotels; Lauterbrunnen – hotels, dormitory accommodation, camping

Once again there are numerous options available to those who would choose to shorten this stage, either by spending a night at an intermediate location, or taking some form of transport. It's a stage that will rarely be walked in solitude. The crowds thronging Grindelwald and Kleine Scheidegg and the year-round popularity of Wengen ensure that the area will be busy when you pass through. Most of the footpaths that lead from one to the other will be well trodden too, and rightly so.

The ascent to Kleine Scheidegg is surprisingly steep. When you first look up at the saddle it's difficult to believe that there is more than 1000m of altitude difference, yet almost as soon as you leave Grund (in the bed of Grindelwald's valley) you will understand that this is to be no easy stroll. But make the most of the close proximity of the Eiger from Alpiglen onwards, and look forward to the early part of the descent as far as Wengen, for the views of Mönch and Jungfrau will more than repay the effort of the ascent.

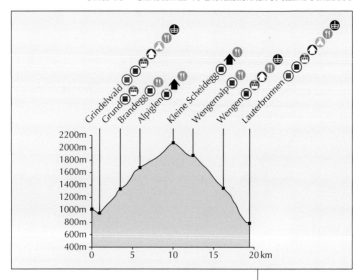

From **Grindelwald** railway station follow signs that direct you downhill to the station at **Grund** (943m, **15min**, railways, shops and Eigergletscher and Mannlichen cable cars). From here cross the railway line and a bridge over the Schwarze Lütschine river, veer left through parking to find a steep tarmac path that climbs between meadows and houses, signed to Alpiglen and Kleine Scheidegg. It maintains its steep gradient nearly all the way to Alpiglen, but above the initial group of chalets and farms there are open meadows, the way often rising parallel to the cog railway with backward views to the Wetterhorn, and the Eiger rising over your left shoulder. The first hour is on tarmac, then you go through woods and past the station at **Brandegg** (restaurant, refreshments, 1332m), and from there along a track which leads to the tiny station and group of buildings at **Alpiglen** (1616m, **2hr 15min**).

Berghaus Alpiglen 12 beds, 40 dormitory places, refreshments available (tel 033 853 11 30, www.alpiglen.ch).

Many **Eigerwand climbers** have set out from Alpiglen to attempt the stark north wall that soars above the pastures to the south, and a number of these never returned. Trekkers, however, can enjoy Alpiglen's hospitality without that challenge and, seated at the hotel terrace with a cool drink before you and your back to the Eiger, is to be treated to a grandstand view of the toy-like buildings of Grindelwald, with the Wetterhorn its dominant backdrop.

Grindelwald and the Wetterhorn viewed from near Männlichen

A short way beyond the **Alpiglen** berghaus cross the railway line and follow the broad track that eases uphill beneath the Eiger's North Face towards the large hotel buildings of **Kleine Scheidegg** (2061m) that appear deceptively close. It will take almost 1hr 30min from Alpiglen to get there (**3hr 45min**).

Kleine Scheidegg Accommodation, refreshments, railway station. Lower-priced accommodation (including dormitories) at the Bahnhof Restaurant (tel 033 828 78 88, www.bergrestaurant-kleine-scheidegg.ch), and 10min along the path towards Männlichen, Restaurant Grindelwaldblick has six rooms and 60 dormitory places in four rooms (tel 033 855 13 74, www.grindelwaldblick.ch).

The classic view of a train headed for the spectacular viewpoint at the Jungfraujoch at near 4000m

This much-visited, much-publicised **viewpoint** in the shadow of Eiger, Mönch and Jungfrau, is a major junction on the Jungfraujoch railway. As such it suffers from a rash of development not altogether in keeping with a high mountain environment. Clapham Junction at 2000m? Not quite, but the clutter of buildings, excitable crowds, souvenir kiosks and alpenhorns make it one of the busiest crossings on the VA. Perhaps recognising its potential, Christian Seiler built the first hotel here in 1834, while construction of the Jungfraujoch Railway (1896–1912) effectively sealed its fate.

THE EIGER

The mountain has passed into notoriety far beyond the confined world of the climbing fraternity (for whom its horrors have faded somewhat) on account of numerous tragedies played out on its North Face, beginning in the 1930s. The first ascent of this 3970m peak was made, not via the North Face, but by its south-east flank by Charles Barrington, with the guides Christian Almer and Peter Bohren, on 11 August 1858. The graceful knife-ridge of the Mittellegi was ascended in 1921 by the Japanese climber Yuko Maki and his

guides, while the North Face (Nordwand) was only completed in 1938 by Harrer, Kasparek, Heckmair and Vörg. The face has since been climbed in winter, solo, by siege tactics, and under 2hr 30min by Swiss speed climber Ueli Steck. See *The White Spider* by Heinrich Harrer (Hart-Davis, 1959) and *The Eiger* by Dougal Haston (Cassell, 1974) for well-documented histories of climbing on the North Face.

Cross the railway line to the left of the main station buildings and descend a broad path (signed to Wengernalp and Wengen), which mostly parallels the railway. The Mönch and Jungfrau provide a sublime distraction from the less-pleasing aspects of overhead power lines and crowded passing trains. At **Wengernalp** (hotel, refreshments) there is a further opportunity to take a train to Wengen and Lauterbrunnen.

WENGERNALP

'Surely the Wengern Alp must be precisely the loveliest place in this world,' wrote Leslie Stephen in *The Playground of Europe* (Longman, 1871). 'It is delicious to lie upon the short crisp turf under the Lauberhorn, to listen to the distant cowbells, and try to catch the moment at which the last glow dies off the summit of the Jungfrau.' Stephen, and others since, also mentioned the avalanches that pour from the face of the Jungfrau almost hourly in summer, and which can be safely observed from the Wengernalp pastures. 'The avalanche, as it descends from rock to rock on the mountain-side, to disappear at its foot,' said Baedeker in one of his early guides to Switzerland, 'resembles a huge white cascade.' Because it lies near the Wengen to Kleine Scheidegg railway, the Wengernalp is much better known than the neighbouring Biglenalp and Mettlenalp, both of which share similar views but are more peaceful, despite being easily reached by footpaths from Wengernalp itself.

The VA follows the line of the railway virtually all the way to **Wengen** (1276m, **5hr 30min**). In fact, the railway impinges little on the walk and the views are fine throughout. An optional route via Mettlenalp could be considered for those keen for quieter trails.

The attractive resort of Wengen

WENGEN (1276M)

Located on a comfortably wide terrace 500m above the Lauterbrunnen valley, Wengen is a popular car-free summer and winter resort with outstanding views over the classic U-shaped, glacier-carved valley, and to the Jungfrau, Mittaghorn, Breithorn and Tschingelhorn at its head. Known to botanists for its wealth of alpine flowers in spring and early summer, its fame these days is perhaps focused on the World Cup downhill- and slalom- ski races held on the Lauberhorn each January. On the wrong side of the valley to be a favourite overnight stop on the VA, its restaurants offer welcome refreshment on the way through.

Tourist information (tel 033 855 14 14, www.wengen.com). Hotels, gasthofs, restaurants, shops, banks, post office, railway connections with destinations including Lauterbrunnen, Interlaken and Grindelwald. Lower-priced accommodation: Hotel Brunner (tel 033 855 24 94, www.brunner-hotel.com), Hotel Falken (tel 033 856 51 21, www.hotelfalken.com).

A descent route to Lauterbrunnen is signed from Wengen railway station. It cuts beneath the railway line and leads onto a narrow road. A path soon breaks away then twists down through steep mixed forest, crosses the railway on two occasions, gives occasional views between the trees to the Staubbach Falls, and eventually crosses a footbridge over the Weisse Lütschine just before climbing to the station, which it passes underneath, to enter **Lauterbrunnen** (**6hr 30min**). Lauterbrunnen Dorf is 400m left from the station.

Looking down into the deep Lauterbrunnen valley; Mürren is on the shelf across the valley

LAUTERBRUNNEN (800M)

A somewhat straggling resort, Lauterbrunnen is built where the narrow valley of the Weisse Lütschine begins to open out, and takes its name from the many waterfalls that cascade down the near-vertical cliffs that line the valley. The best of these is the Staubbach, a 300m smoky thread in a dry summer, but an impressive spout following heavy rainfall. The prettiest building is the church near the southern end of the village, where a large bell in the churchyard is said to have been carried over the glacier pass of the Wetterlücke several centuries ago, in a mass migration from the Lötschental in canton Valais.

Tourist information (tel 033 856 85 68, www.lauterbrunnen.swiss). Hotels, gasthofs, two campsites, shops, restaurants, bank, post office, rail connections with Interlaken, Wengen, Kleine Scheidegg and Grindelwald; cable car and train to Mürren via Grütschalp, bus to Mürren via Stechelberg and the Schilthornbahn cable car. Lower-priced accommodation: Backpackers Valley Hostel (dormitories, tel 033 855 20 08, www.valleyhostel.ch); dormitories are also available at the campsites, Jungfrau (tel 033 856 20 10, www.campingjungfrau.swiss) and Schützenbach Backpackers & Camping (tel 033 855 12 68, www.schutzenbach. ch). Hotel Horner (tel 033 855 16 73, www.hornerpub.ch), Hotel Staubbach (tel 033 855 54 54, www.staubbach.ch).

Route options between Grindelwald and Wengen

The Grindelwald/Wengen area is one of the leading Alpine walking areas. As well as the train/cable car options, this gives the VA trekker many options to vary the route, which include (amongst many options):

- Taking the high route to Alpiglen. From Grindelwald take paths to Gletscherschlucht and climb steeply with views of the gorge. Continue climbing, signed to Alpiglen and cross the Schüssellauenen, which drains the Mittellegi ridge of the Eiger. Follow the high trail and descend to Alpiglen. Allow 4hr from Grindelwald to Alpiglen.
- This route can be combined with staying at Hotel Wetterhorn on Stage 9, taking either lower paths to Marmorbruch and Gletscherschlucht, or a higher route via the Pfinstegg top station. Allow 5–6hr from Hotel Wetterhorn to Alpiglen.
- From Alpiglen, take the Eiger Trail to Eigergletscher beneath the rocks of the Eiger and then drop down to Kleine Scheidegg. Allow 3hr.
- Take the cable car to Männlichen and walk the 1hr route to Kleine Scheidegg with face-on views to the Eiger North Face.
- From Wengernalp, explore the Mettlenalp trails, with close-up views of both the Mönch and Jungfrau, rejoining the route after Stalden, adding an additional hour to the descent into Wengen.

Staying in Mürren

In view of the length of the next stage, and the fact that more than 1800m of height will have to be gained to reach the Sefinenfurgga, it might be considered worthwhile continuing up to Mürren for the night – by bus and cable car via Stechelberg, or cable car to Grütschalp and then train or footpath from there. To walk the extra 2hr 30min from Lauterbrunnen at the end of a day that began in Grindelwald would make for a very long day, especially in view of the rigours to come over the next days. Another strong reason why a night spent at or near Mürren could be worthwhile is the opportunity to witness the Jungfrau catching the blush of alpenglow, and watching dawn rise over Eiger, Mönch and Jungfrau from a terrace high above the Lauterbrunnental (valley). (See Stage 11 for accommodation details.)

STAGE 11

Lauterbrunnen to Griesalp by the Sefinafurgga

Start	Lauterbrunnen 800m
Finish	Griesalp 1408m
Distance	22.5km
Total ascent	1910m
Total descent	1300m
Time	9hr 15min
High point(s)	Sefinafurgga 2611m
Maps	LS 5004 Berner Oberland; K&F 18 Jungfrau Region
Transport	Cable car (Lauterbrunnen–Grütschalp); train (Grütschalp–Mürren); Bus to Stechelberg and cable car (Schilthornbahn) to Mürren
Accommodation	Mürren (2hr 30min) – hotels, and pensions; Blumental (3hr) – pensions with dormitory accommodation; Spielbodenalp (3hr 10min) – pension with dormitory accommodation; Rotstock Hut (4hr 45min), dormitory accommodation; Griesalp – hotels

Crossing the Sefinafurgga (or Sefinenfurgge), the trek leaves the busy tourist areas of the Bernese Oberland and enters a wilder, more remote region. The pass is the highest of the route so far, with a long but straightforward approach, and a steep climb for the final 150m on shale to reach the col, with steps protecting the final section of the col climb. The shale continues on the western side of the pass, but with a much longer wooden staircase to ease the descent.

Yet again it's a long day's trek. However, as indicated in Stage 10, by taking transport options from Lauterbrunnen to Mürren, some 2hr 30min of stern uphill effort could be saved, making the remainder of the walk a little less demanding. Purists unhappy with the thought of this amount of mechanical aid might consider a compromise by taking the cable car to Grütschalp and walking from there – a lovely scenic walk. (Mürren is reached in 1hr 10min from Grütschalp, thus saving almost 1hr 30min on the day's overall time and reducing the height gain by a little over 700m.)

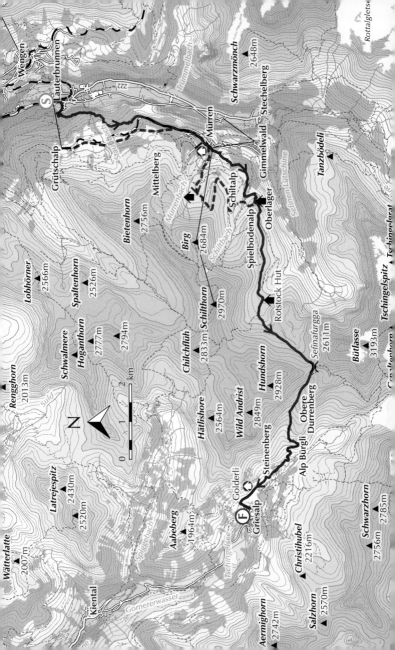

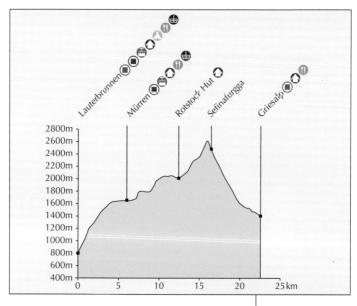

The path to Mürren is located by the Jungfrau Garage in **Lauterbrunnen**'s main street where a sign suggests 2hr 30min for the ascent. At first the way climbs very steeply by the Gryfenbach stream, but on coming to a junction you take the left branch, slanting less severely now uphill through forest with occasional views between the trees. There are several streams to cross, including the Staubbach, and across the valley the Jungfrau looks magnificent, seen in all its glory from its roots in the Lauterbrunnental to its pristine snow-gleaming summit – an altitude difference of more than 3200m. After a little over 2hr the Grütschalp–Mürren railway is joined near **Mittelberg** (1611m), and

The Jungfrau and lower Lauterbrunnen valley

there you turn left and a little under 30min later arrive in **Mürren** (1638m, **2hr 30min**).

MÜRREN (1638M)

Said to be the highest permanently inhabited village in the Bernese Oberland, Mürren, like Wengen on the other side of the Lauterbrunnen valley, occupies an idyllic shelf some 800m above the valley floor, and is a very popular car-free resort noted for its views. It was first recorded in the 13th century as Mons Mürren, and in the first half of the 19th was visited by several notable Englishmen, including John Addington Symonds and Lord Tennyson. But it was Arnold Lunn who accelerated its year-round popularity when he invented the modern slalom there in 1922. Two years later he founded the Kandahar Ski Club at the Palace Hotel, and in 1928 the 'Inferno' ski race from the Schilthorn to Lauterbrunnen (a descent of 2170m) had its first outing. It continues as an annual event each February. A memorial stone dedicated to Lunn stands in a small garden by the railway station.

Tourist information (tel 033 856 86 86, www.muerren.ch). Hotels, pensions, restaurants, shops, banks, post office. Lower-priced accommodation: Pension Suppenalp (beds and dormitory places, tel 033 855 17 26, www.suppenalp.ch), Pension Sonnenberg (beds and dormitory places, tel 033 855 11 27, www.restaurant-sonnenberg.ch), Pension Spielbodenalp (Friday to Sunday only; beds and dormitory places, tel 079 646 91 16), Hotel Bellevue (tel 033 855 14 01, www.bellevuemuerren.ch), Hotel Regina (tel 033 855 42 42, www.reginamuerren.ch), Eiger Guesthouse (tel 033 856 54 60, www.eigerguesthouse.com).

Leaving Mürren station, take the lower of two roads ahead which lead through the village, passing hotels, shops and chalets, all of which enjoy the same fine views. Continue past the Schilthorn cable car station. The road soon starts to climb steeply and after 400 metres and a hairpin bend, take a left turn by a barn. This crosses meadows and woods from which the Breithorn (at the head of the Lauterbrunnental) and Gspaltenhorn (ahead) hold your attention. Drop down to cross the Schiltbach and come to **Pension Spielbodenalp** (1791m, **3hr 15min**, Friday to Sunday only; beds and dormitory places, tel 079 646 91 16).

The continuing path now tackles the short but steep Wasenegg spur by a series of steep zigzags then at the

top of the slope, just below the minor point of Bryndli come to some bench seats (2024m) where the trail forks. Keep left at the Bryndli junction and right at the next junction (in 300m) and contour round the hillside into a large pastureland where you come to the Oberlager junction (2052m). The higher alternative route rejoins here. Continue on a level path to the **Rotstock Hut** (2039m, **4hr 45min**).

The Rotstock Hut provides accommodation and refreshments just over 2hr after Mürren

> **Rotstock Hut** Accommodation, refreshments, 52 dormitory places, open June–October (tel 033 855 24 64, www.rotstockhuette.ch).

THE SCHILTHORN

Mürren's local mountain gave a popular ascent long before the cable car provided ready access to anyone who could afford a ticket. At 2970m, the peak stands just far enough away from the major summits to make a first-rate viewpoint from which to survey a realm of dramatic mountains. The panorama stretches far beyond the immediate wonderland of Eiger, Mönch, Jungfrau and their neighbours, for it is claimed you can also see the Matterhorn and Mont Blanc in a seemingly endless vista. The revolving 'Piz Gloria' summit restaurant was featured in the James Bond film *On Her Majesty's Secret Service*, and scenes from the film are shown in a basement theatre there. (The bizarre nature of this summit entertainment is especially striking if you've made the ascent on foot!)

The steep upper slopes of the Sefinafurgga after early autumn snow

Ahead lies a large basin of rough grass and rocks, on the western side of which the final ascent to the pass begins. The path makes its way over old moraine banks with the Sefinafurgga seen ahead long before you reach it. The last part of the climb ascends a steep zigzag route over slopes of gritty black shale and scree assisted by wooden steps in the top 100 metres to arrive on the **Sefinafurgga** (2611m, **6hr 15min**), about 1hr 30min after leaving the Rotstock Hut.

A long set of steps greatly assists the steep descent after the Sefinafurgga

So different from recent passes crossed on the VA, this is a narrow, craggy dip in a ridge running from the Hundshorn in the north, to the Bütlassa in the south. (This latter peak is connected to the Gspaltenhorn by a short linking ridge.) Turning back for a last eastward glance, both Eiger and Mönch, though far off, hold their stature, while in the opposite direction (if you go round the rocks to the left)

the glacier-hung Blümlisalp massif signals a major presence only a comparatively short distance ahead to the south-west. On Stage 12 our route crosses just below its highest summits.

The steep descent on the western side of the pass is notable for a seemingly endless stairway of steps, avoiding what had previously been a potentially dangerous slope of shale and grit. A cable usually helps the descent but may not always be in place or it could be loose on the ground, making the descent more awkward. Below the stairway a good path descends yet more shale before grassy hillocks take over, with a small stream breaking through a gully on your left. Following this down, a little over an hour from the pass you come to the small farm building of **Obere Dürrenberg** (1996m, **7hr 15min**).

Below the farm, cross to the left bank of the stream where the path winds down a steep hillside under the gaze of the Blümlisalp. The alp farms of Untere and Oberi Bundalp can be seen across the valley to the west, appearing small and remote – these will be visited on the next stage of the route to the Hohtürli. On reaching the farm of **Burgli** (1616m), bear right across the Dürrenberg stream and follow the farm road which

The Bernese Oberland 'mountain wall' – Wetterhorn, Eiger, Mönch and Jungfrau

123

leads down to Griesalp. However, should it be your intention to stay overnight at Oberi Bundalp (on the route of Stage 12), look out for a trail junction just above the pretty hamlet of **Steinenberg** (1467m, **8hr 45min**). Here a signpost directs an alternative waymarked path over a bridge and on to Bundalp (see Alternative route from Berggasthaus Golderli in Stage 12). Continuing on the main route to Griesalp, shortly after passing Steinenberg come to **Golderli** (1440m, **9hr**).

> **Berggasthaus Golderli** Beds and dormitory places, open all year (tel 033 676 21 92, www.golderli. ch). Five minutes ahead and above it you will find **Naturfreundehaus Gorneren** (1471m, tel 033 676 11 40, www.gorneren.nfh.ch).

The road forks here. Take the left branch and follow this through fields and woods for a few minutes down to **Griesalp** (1408m, **9hr 15min**).

GRIESALP (1410M)

This is a tiny hamlet ranged around a square at the end of a narrow toll road that rises through the gentle Kiental valley. Small, specially built postbuses serve the hamlet from Kiental village, on what is said to be Europe's steepest postbus route. With the Tschingelsee below, spectacular high mountain scenery above, accessible neighbouring valleys, and some tough pass crossings to challenge, Griesalp makes a fine base for a walking, climbing or ski-mountaineering holiday away from the bustle of larger Oberland resorts with their international appeal.

For accommodation there's a complex of no fewer than five non-budget hotels: the Berghaus, Grand, Griesschlüchtli, Raspintli and Kurhaus Hohtürli (tel 033 676 71 71, www.griesalp-hotels.ch). The mountain inn at nearby Golderli is the preferable place to stay if taking the alternative route to Oberi Bundalp in Stage 12.

Alternative routes
There are several options for the section into and around Mürren to take advantage of the view of the Eiger and Jungfrau:

Lauterbrunnen to Mürren via Grütschalp (1hr 10min walking). From **Lauterbrunnen** take the cable car to **Grütschalp**, then turn left to find a path just above the railway line, which you follow all the way to Mürren. It's a gently undulating path which gains a little under 150m over 4km. Refreshments are available at Winteregg (1580m), about 30min along the path, and for much of the way views are splendid. The path joins with the main route and enters **Mürren** by the railway station at the northern end of the resort.

One minute beyond the buildings, a narrow path breaks away half-left and contours round the hillside. Continue on the track for about 8min, then turn sharp left at a signpost to descend on a narrow path which soon crosses the **Schiltbach** stream. Take the steeply climbing path among lush, dank vegetation, to emerge on the crest of the narrow grass ridge of Wasenegg at 2155m, with fine panoramic views. The path veers right here and makes an easy-angled descent into a broad pastureland, where you come to another path junction marked as **Oberlager** (**2hr 30min** from Mürren). Here join the main VA route from Mürren for the Rotstock Hut and the Sefinafurgga.

Mürren to Oberlager via the Blumental and Schiltalp (**2hr 30min**). From **Mürren** station take the upper, right-hand road leading into the village, passing the Allmendhubel funicular on the right. Continue ahead until a broad tarmac path branches right, signed to the Blumental. The way winds steeply uphill between houses to enter a picturesque bowl of pasture below the Schilthorn. After passing a few barns, about 30min from Mürren station, you reach Pension Sonnenberg (1840m). At a junction here turn left, and a few minutes later come to Pension Suppenalp, a dairy farm with rustic accommodation and outstanding views of the Jungfrau.

Pass in front of the building and take a path which climbs a vegetated spur to gain a direct view of the impressive Gspaltenhorn, before entering an upper pastureland. Across this the trail leads to **Schiltalp** (1948m), a collection of cheesemakers' huts about 30min from Suppenalp. ▶

It's possible to buy refreshments here.

STAGE 12
Griesalp to Kandersteg by the Hohtürli

Start	Griesalp 1408m
Finish	Kandersteg 1170m
Distance	18km
Total ascent	1460m (including Blümlisalp Hut)
Total descent	1700m
Time	7hr 30min
High point(s)	Hohtürli 2778m; Blümlisalp Hut 2835m
Maps	LS 5004 Berner Oberland; K&F 18 Jungfrau Region
Transport	Gondola lift (Oeschinensee–Kandersteg)
Accommodation	Oberi Bundalp (1hr 15min) – berggasthof with dormitory accommodation; Hohtürli (4hr) – Blümlisalp Hut (SAC hut with dormitory accommodation); Oeschinensee (6hr 30min) – hotel and berghaus with dormitory accommodation; Kandersteg – hotels, gasthofs, dormitories, camping

The Hohtürli is the highest point on the Via Alpina (apart from the Blümlisalp Hut located 60m above it), and its crossing is one of the most demanding. That being said, it's one to look forward to and enjoy. The route is varied, beginning with a woodland walk before joining a farm road that winds easily uphill among pastures, followed by a sudden upward climb that tackles a steep spur of scree and shale to a minor ridge. Beyond that, a rising traverse leads to a long flight of well-constructed wooden steps and chains to facilitate the ascent of an abrupt slope leading directly to the pass.

The Hohtürli is a grandstand from which to view a wild mountain landscape, as untamed as anything witnessed since leaving Sargans. Small glaciers hang from the Blümlisalp massif, while the deep Kandersteg valley is but a shadow far below a confusion of moraine crests, screes and converging ridges. The descent takes you down those screes and along moraine spurs, before gaining a grassy basin from which you gaze into the fjord-like well that contains the Oeschinensee. A belvedere of a trail skirts the lake's north shore, while the final descent is down a steep forested slope that spills out into Kandersteg, with an option to take the cable car. It's a great day's walk, tough but rewarding.

Looking at the long ascent of the Hohtürli

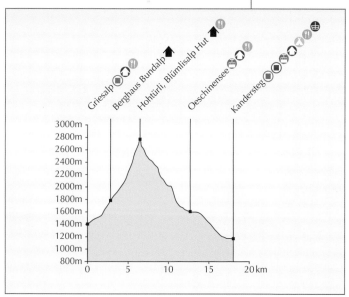

127

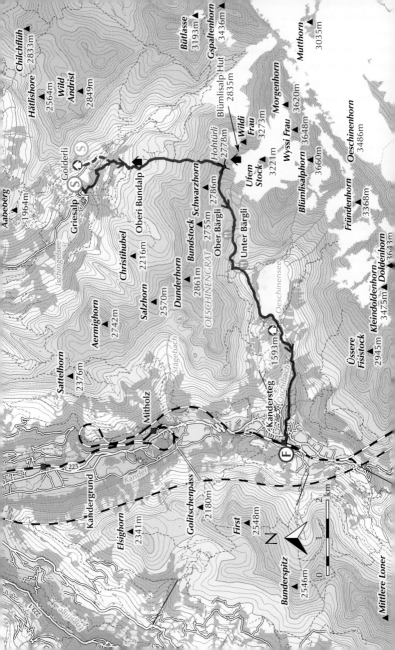

At **Griesalp** a signpost by a map board indicates the start of the walk to the Hohtürli. Take the path which rises through woodland to a farm road, and there turn left. While it would be possible to follow this road all the way to (and beyond) Oberi Bundalp, signs and waymarks lead to a footpath short cut. This leaves the road just before a sharp bend, cuts to the left and heads through forest and pasture, crosses streams and eventually rejoins the road where it winds through the Bundalp pastureland near Underi Bundalp (1690m). Leave the road again and take the continuing path which rises to a higher shelf of pastureland where you come onto the road once more, shortly before reaching **Oberi Bundalp** (1841m, **1hr 15min**).

OBERI BUNDALP (1841M)

Oberi Bundalp enjoys great views of the surrounding peaks. To the north-east, the Schilthorn and Wetterhorn are easily recognisable. To the west, a confusion of ridges block the main wall of Oberland peaks, but the Blümlisalp massif with its shrinking glacier is the main object of attention, for it dominates the view from the pass you're aiming for.

Berghaus Bundalp offers refreshments, beds and dormitory accommodation, open mid-June–end September (tel 033 676 11 92, www.bundalp.ch).

Alternative route: Berggasthaus Golderli to Oberi Bundalp (1hr 15min)

Walkers who stayed overnight at Berggasthaus **Golderli** have no need to descend to Griesalp to join the Hohtürli route, for a very pleasant series of paths link forest and pasture before coming onto the farm road at Untere Bundalp.

Retracing the last part of Stage 11, walk back to Steinenberg (1470m), then take a signed path to the right through meadows and woodland. About 15min from Golderli, cross the Gamchibach and come onto another path which began in Griesalp. Go up the slope, then more steeply in zigzags through forest to gain the open alp pastures of Untere Bundalp (1690m) and a farm road. Take the continuing path up through the pastures to rejoin the road just before reaching **Oberi Bundalp**.

Main route

Keep along the road for a few minutes, then break to the right on a signed path that rises over more rough pastureland to a steep slope of moraine deposits, partly grassed over. Working a way up a spur of black grit (slippery after rain) the slope is surprisingly severe, and erosion by rain and snow provides many path options – runnels and gullies have been washed out by successive spring thaws and heavy rainfall. However, the severity of the slope means that height is gained with practically every step, and when you pause for a rest, views are rewarding – the Thunersee gleams in the distant north, while the Blümlisalp Hut can be seen on the ridge above to the south.

The slope of black moraine ends on a grey rock ridge, and the way then makes a short rising traverse before tucking against its left-hand (east) side. The ascent steepens again, with fixed cables and a long succession of timber steps beneath overhanging crags. Then at last you emerge onto the **Hohtürli** (2778m, **3hr 45min**) to be greeted by a panorama of wild beauty.

Just above the pass, about 15min walk away, stands the **Blümlisalp Hut** (2835m, **4hr**). ◄

The hut is being renovated and will be closed in 2023 and is planned to reopen in 2024.

The Blümlisalp Hut is 60m above the Hohtürli; it is reached around lunchtime

Blümlisalp Hut Owned by the Thun-based Blümlisalp section of the SAC, 117 places, guardian in residence end June–mid-October during which time refreshments are available (tel 033 676 14 37, www.bluemlisalphuette.com).

BLÜMLISALP

The fine, snowy massif of Blümlisalp dominates the route between Griesalp and Kandersteg. There are three main summits of more than 3600m, each with its own hanging glacier feeding onto the Blümlisalpgletscher on the north flank, and with short but steep walls on the south side dropping to the Kanderfirn icefield. The massif's highest summit is the Blümlisalphorn (3657m), first climbed in August 1860. Next is the Wyssi Frau (3648m), followed by the Morgenhorn (3620m) which rises above the Blümlisalp Hut, but is partly obscured by the 3260m Wilde Frau – a noted viewpoint easily climbed from the hut.

The way down to Kandersteg is on a clearly marked path, initially on well-graded zigzags over broad slopes of scree. It has none of the fierce steepness of the ascent. It crosses a single-file bridge over a ravine, then descends to a balcony in view of glacier-smoothed slabs. ▶ Descending still, you come onto the crest of a

There are dramatic views across to the Blümlisalp's glaciers, impressive despite being much smaller than in the past.

131

moraine wall, before veering to the right into a rough bowl of pastureland littered with rocks and boulders. Here you come to the huts of **Ober Bärgli** (1978m, **5hr 45min**, refreshments).

Shortly after this, you come to the edge of a precipice and gaze down into the fjord-like basin of the Oeschinensee.

> **Oeschinensee** is one of the most notable mountain lakes in Switzerland; a beautiful, oval sheet of water cupped in a great amphitheatre of mountains at over 1500m, and accessed by gondola lift (and a 20min walk) from Kandersteg. The peaks of the Blümlisalp and Dündenhorn rise abruptly from its shoreline, while the western end tilts steeply among forest down to the Kandertal. The lake is not only a natural focus for visitors to Kandersteg, but marks the start of some challenging walks, among them the 1000m ascent to the Fründen Hut. (See *100 Hut Walks in the Alps* [Cicerone Press].)

The path now descends a stony track slanting down a cliff, at the foot of which you reach the alp of **Unter Bärgli** (1767m, refreshments usually available in summer). Bear right here, cross a stream on a footbridge, and follow the continuing path which now leads along the north side of the lake, but still some way above it.

FOLLOWING THE CATTLE HOME

It was the end of summer and all the cattle and goats were being driven from the alps, where they'd been grazing since June, down to the lowlands. The lead cows had their heads adorned with flowers and wreaths and with tiny trees fixed to their horns. They led the procession with a strange kind of bovine dignity, while one or two of the goats played truant and tried to escape by climbing above the path. A well-aimed stone from one of the herders checked the error of their ways and they returned to their rightful place near the back of the line. We strolled behind them, unable to overtake, walking on a moist brown carpet all the way to the lake's end.

Towards the western end of the lake the path slopes down to ease through woodland along the shoreline, passes a number of carved figures and animals on tree stumps, and eventually comes out to a couple of hotels overlooking the **Oeschinensee** (1593m, **6hr 30min**).

The Oeschinensee with the Blümlisalp above

> Refreshments, beds and dormitory places at both the **Berghotel Oeschinensee** (tel 033 675 11 19, www. oeschinensee.ch), and **Berghaus am Oeschinensee** (tel 033 675 11 66, www.arva-oeschinensee.ch).

The final descent to Kandersteg takes about an hour, but should you be weary from the day's efforts so far, it's possible to take the gondola, a 20min walk from the hotels, which will deposit you by the Kandersteg campsite. Better still, spend the night at Oeschinensee.

The route to Kandersteg is currently impacted by cable car and water/river-management works, so may be changed. Continue ahead on a service road looking out for footpaths off to the right, descending steeply in places. The road passes several waterfalls coming from the left. As you lose height there are alternative options to consider, depending on your plans for the night. For the campsite (which also has dormitory accommodation) follow signs for the gondola, but for other accommodation follow directions for the *bahnhof* (railway station). As you approach the town routes either side of the Öschibach may be signed. About 1hr from the Oeschinensee, you arrive in **Kandersteg** (1170m, **7hr 30min**).

KANDERSTEG (1170M)

Kandersteg has long been used as a mountaineering centre and a base for walking holidays. (See *The Bernese Oberland* [Cicerone Press], a walking guide which includes a selection of routes.) There is much fine scenery on all sides, some delightful accessible valleys, high passes to cross (glaciated and ice free), and a number of mountain huts placed within a few hours' walk of the village centre. A major International Scout Camp is located at the southern end of the village, while the public campsite is situated on the eastern outskirts at the foot of the Oeschinen gondola lift.

Tourist information (tel 033 675 80 80, www.kandersteg.ch). Hotels, pensions, campsite, restaurants, shops, bank, post office, rail connections to destinations including Spiez, Interlaken and Brig. Lower-priced accommodation: Camping Rendezvous (tel 033 675 15 34, www.camping-kandersteg.ch), Hotel zur Post (tel 033 675 12 58,) and Hotel des Alpes (tel 033 675 11 12, www.desalpes-kandersteg.ch).

STAGE 13

Kandersteg to Adelboden by the Bunderchrinde

Start	Kandersteg 1170m
Finish	Adelboden 1350m
Distance	17.5km
Total ascent	1480m
Total descent	1300m
Time	7hr
High point(s)	Bunderchrinde 2382m
Maps	LS 5009 Gstaad–Adelboden; K&F 18 Jungfrau Region and 32 Crans-Montana
Transport	Cable car (Kandersteg–Allmenalp – off route)
Accommodation	Bonderalp (5hr 20min) – berghaus with dormitory accommodation; Adelboden – hotels, pensions, campsites; Boden (6hr 30min) – hotel, pension, dormitory accommodation

Bunderchrinde is the last of the classic mountain passes of the VA, a mere nick in the high craggy ridge that extends from the Gross Lohner to the Allmegrat and effectively separates the Kandertal from the Engstligental. On the Kandersteg side the route ascends in steps, from one natural shelf to the next. First there's an easy meadowland walk, then a steep climb through woodland to gain the Üschene hanging valley. Here there's another gentle interlude before rising steeply again, this time to overcome a long line of slabs and cliffs from which views open into the lovely Gasterntal to the south-east. Above these cliffs you traverse a shelf of rough pasture to the Alpschele huts, before tackling the final scree slope that leads to the Bunderchrinde. The downward path similarly descends in steps and takes almost as long to complete as the upward section.

From the centre of the village, take the road west to **Kandersteg** railway station where a signpost directs you left along a tarmac footpath following the railway line heading south. The way soon veers right under a bridge, crosses the River Kander and goes along a narrow road towards the landing site of the Kandersteg paragliding

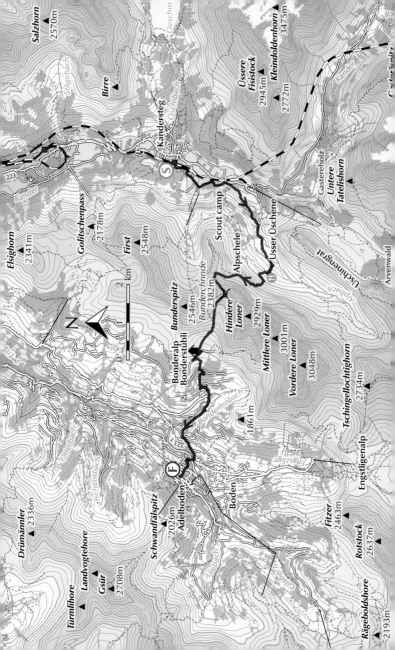

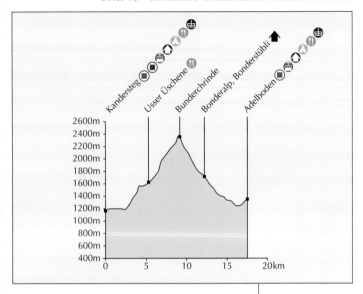

school. ▸ From here a path continues beside the river and brings you to the **International Scout Camp**, Pfadfinder Zentrum (1186m, **30min**). A few paces beyond the main building a footpath breaks away to the right and sends you across meadows.

The Allmenalp cable car is just off route, taking you to 1725m, also somewhat off route.

Midway across one of these meadows the path forks. Take the right branch into woods where the ascent begins, the path now rising steeply to a road. Cross this and continue through more woodland before coming onto the road once more. Follow the road uphill for 5min until it makes a right-hand hairpin, at which point you go ahead on a waymarked path rising above the Alpbach stream. This rejoins the road at another hairpin where once again you go ahead on a narrow path climbing through a gorge to arrive in the open pastures of **Usser Üschene** (1548m, **1hr 15min**) where a sign indicates the way to the Bunderchrinde in 2hr 20min.

Continue directly ahead across the pastures, keeping below the main alp buildings (one of which – Restaurant

Lohner – offers summer refreshments). At the far end of the pastures you come to a junction of farm tracks and take the upper right option that winds uphill. Just before it comes to an alp building (about 30min from Usser Üschene) take a path on the left, which climbs towards a band of grey cliffs.

The path swings to the left, crosses a stream and resumes the ascent, seeking a fault line up the cliffs. Recrossing the stream the path zigzags steeply before heading to the right over boulder slopes with views south-east to the Gasterntal.

Feeding into the head of the Kandertal east of Kandersteg, the **Gasterntal** is a magnificent, steep-walled valley sliced by meandering streams born either among the Kanderfirn glacier, or by the numerous waterfalls that streak the great rock faces. There are no villages in the valley, just a hotel, a couple of rustic inns and a handful of farm buildings, but it's an enchanting place well worth a visit should you have sufficient days to spare. Failing that, make a point of returning to Kandersteg on another occasion in order to explore this rewarding 'back of beyond'.

Light refreshments are sometimes available here in high summer.

Eventually come to the three simple huts of **Alpschele** (2087m, **3hr**) from where you can see the Bunderchrinde above. ◄

LOCAL HOSPITALITY

Treading knee-high clouds and hunched against the cold rain on one of my early crossings of the VA, two of us arrived at Alpschele and were invited inside the main hut to dry off. Seated on their bed, we were given tall glasses of milky coffee by the cheesemakers who lived there for the summer. Remembering them with affection, when I returned the following year I was hopeful of a similar welcome. But this time summer was virtually over and the cheesemakers had gone down to the valley. My heart fell. In their place were two chamois hunters who nonetheless sympathised with us (it was another

The top of the scree descent from the Bunderchrinde

cold and blustery day), and who were every bit as hospitable as had been their predecessors, for they presented us with bowls of what they called Jäger Kaffee (Hunters' Coffee) – milk coffee laced with apfelschnapps – to combat the cold. It was very effective, and when we set off again along the path our cheeks had a healthy glow that had nothing to do with the effort of walking.

The path rises between the buildings, then makes a steady rising traverse to the right across an increasingly stony hillside, before winding up to a junction of paths and a signpost on the edge of a broad slope of scree. The way slants across the scree at a comfortable gradient initially with a final steep section, and brings you directly to the splendid narrow gap of the **Bunderchrinde** (2382m, **4hr**).

The descent begins very steeply and takes zigzags over steep screes, but soon the angle lessens as the path heads towards a grassy bluff at the foot of a stone-scooped corrie in which there's a small cattle byre.

The path descends to the left of this and steepens again as it descends from the high hanging valley.

It crosses rough pasture and is then directed right with marker posts. At a building the path turns left and soon after right at Schrickmatte then continues down. Turn right here for **Bonderalp** (1755m, **5hr 20min**).

> **Berghaus Bonderalp** Open mid-June– mid-September, dormitory places, tel 079 937 54 55, www.berghaus-bonderalp.jimdosite.com. The Bonderstübli mountain inn is 3min further on.

Continue down on the VA route. The way is signed and waymarked (Adelboden 1hr 45min), and descends over pasture and through forest, crossing the road several times and then rejoining it in the valley of the Bunderle Bach. Cross a bridge at 1297m and climb to the road. Keep along the road, passing chalets, before coming to the edge of Adelboden. Turn right at a junction towards a garage, cross the main road and follow yellow *Wanderweg* signs steeply uphill into **Adelboden** (1350m, **7hr**).

Gentle hillsides on the descent into Adelboden

ADELBODEN (1350M)

A summer and winter resort built on a high terrace above its river, with a view of the snowy Wildstrubel to the south, Adelboden enjoys a sunny location at the confluence of several tributary valleys, the best of which is that of the Engstligenalp, whose abundant waterfall can be seen from the village. This waterfall, the Engstligenfälle, has been a Swiss national monument since 1948. Above it there's a charming pastureland with lots of walking opportunities under the Wildstrubel massif. Being quietly fashionable, Adelboden tends to be a little more expensive than some of the other places on the VA.

Tourist information (tel 033 673 80 80, www.adelboden.ch). Hotels, pensions, dormitory accommodation, two campsites, restaurants, shops, banks, post office, bus connections with Frutigen for the Bern–Brig railway line. Lower-priced accommodation: Pension-Restaurant Ruedy-Hus (tel 033 673 33 22); Pension-Restaurant Bodehüttli (beds and dormitory places in nearby Boden – closed Tuesdays and Wednesdays, tel 033 673 37 00, www.bodehuettli-adelboden.ch), Pension Sonne (in Boden, tel 033 673 10 60, www.pensionsonne.ch), Bernerhof B&B (tel 033 673 14 31, www.bernahof.ch); Hotel Crea (tel 062 511 10 11, www.dw-hotels.com/adelboden-hotel-crea).

STAGE 14
Adelboden to Lenk by the Hahnenmoospass

Start	Adelboden 1350m
Finish	Lenk 1064m
Distance	14km
Total ascent	680m
Total descent	970m
Time	4hr 30min
High point(s)	Hahnenmoospass 1950m
Maps	LS 5009 Gstaad–Adelboden; K&F 32 Crans-Montana
Transport	Bus (Adelboden–Geils), gondola (Adelboden–Berglägler), gondola (Adelboden–Berglägler–Sillerenbühl) + 40min walk to Hahnenmoospass, gondola (Geils–Hahnenmoospass), minibus (Büelberg–Lenk), bus (Oberried–Lenk)
Accommodation	Geils (2hr) – restaurant with dormitory accommodation; Hahnenmoospass (2hr 45min) – berghotel with dormitory accommodation; Lenk – hotels, camping

After a number of tough stages, this is an easy day's walk. There are no major ascents or descents, no craggy ridges or screes to tackle, but a welcoming landscape of grass and tree. The route takes tracks and riverside paths, and wanders through meadow and woodland, while the crossing of the broad grass saddle of Hahnenmoos will no doubt be taken in your stride. On the downside, the way is accompanied in several places by mechanical uplift which may detract from your enjoyment of the route's scenic qualities (although these lifts could be welcome if inclement weather deters you from walking all the way).

While the descent to Lenk is direct and straightforward, an alternative route is offered via the Pommernpass and impressive Simmenfälle, which would add 2hr 30min to the overall walk.

Head east from the centre of **Adelboden** and take the signed turn downhill after 3min. Descend between chalets, dropping 80m to cross the river, then immediately

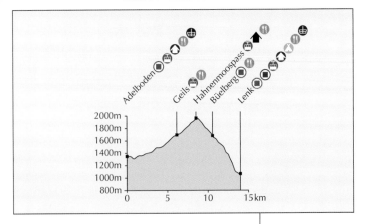

turn right. After 25min reach a confluence of streams (the Gilsbach from the south, **Allebach** from the west) with a road bridge crossing above a small chalet (possible refreshments). Cross the **Gilsbach** and turn left on a broad path climbing beside the river, then cross again to the left-hand side.

The Wildstrubel massif above dominates the southern horizon

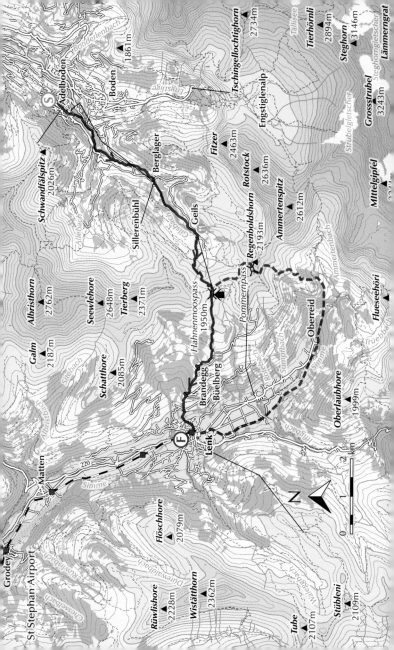

Following the Gilsbach upstream, in 40min come to a narrow road, turn left, and 1min later bear right along a narrow farm road; you are under the gondola lift at this point. The farm road soon curves left, at which point go directly ahead on a path through woodland, then across the Gilsbach once more to **Bergläger** (1485m), the middle station of the Silleren gondola lift.

A narrow, paved road now leads upvalley for about 10min. When it makes a right-hand hairpin, recross the river on a footbridge and continue upstream on a path through woods, then out to open pastures leading directly to **Geils** (1706m, **2hr**).

> **Geils** Also known as Geilsbüel. Gondola to Hahnenmoos, refreshments at Restaurant Geilsbrüggli (tel 033 673 21 71).

Take a minor paved road between the gondola station and the restaurant. This rises easily through pastures, and reaches the **Hahnenmoospass** in about 45min (1950m, **2hr 45min**). Thanks to its accessibility it can be as crowded as the Grosse Scheidegg or Klausenpass on a fine day, but the views, especially to the Wildstrubel, are excellent. ▸

As the pass is a centre for model glider enthusiasts, in good weather gliders can be seen parked up or flying overhead.

> **Hahnenmoospass** Accommodation (rooms and dormitory places) and refreshments at Berghotel Hahnenmoospass (tel 033 673 21 41, www.hahnenmoos.ch).

Ascending the Hahnenmoospass

Obstacles on the path on the descent into Lenk

There are two ways down to Lenk from here. The main VA is given first, while an alternative route via the Pommernpass is described below.

Over the pass veer right onto a track that eases along the hillside in a gentle descent, and in about 30min brings you to **Büelberg** (1660m, **3hr**). Turn right to pass a large restaurant (bus service to Lenk), then take a signed path which descends the hillside, crossing the road several times, with Lenk now seen in the valley below, and the Simmental flowing off to the right.

The way descends to a road at **Brandegg** (1536m), and after passing a number of houses, a sign directs the continuing route along a track on the right, leading to a farm. Beyond this a path continues the descent to Lenk, crossing and recrossing the road with good direction signs or waymarks, descending through flower meadows and brief patches of woodland before merging with a road and entering **Lenk** (1064m, **4hr 30min**).

LENK (1060M)

Originally known as a thermal spa, the small winter and summer resort of Lenk nestles in a flat one-time marshy section of the Simmental, of which it is the highest proper village. Much of the original village was destroyed by fire in 1878, but although there are few really old buildings left, Lenk has developed into a charming resort that makes a good base for a walking holiday. At the head of the valley the Simmenfälle are not the only attraction, for the south-west branch leads to the Iffigtal and a wide range of walking possibilities. The modest green ridge that effectively separates Lenk's valley from that of Lauenen to the west also has numerous trails worth exploring. (See *The Bernese Oberland* [Cicerone Press] for recommended routes.)

Tourist information (tel 033 736 35 35, www.lenk.ch). Hotels, camping, restaurants, bank, post office, rail connections with Zweisimmen and Spiez on the Bern–Brig line. Lower-priced accommodation: the excellent Garni-Hotel Alpina (tel 033 733 10 57, www.alpina-lenk.ch), Garrni-Hotel Alpenruh (tel 033 733 10 64, www.alpenruh-lenk.ch), Mountain Lodge 033 736 30 00). There is also dormitory accommodation at Berghotel Leiterli, near the Trütlisbergpass – see Stage 15 – reached by gondola. After Lenk there are no banks on the Via Alpina variants until you reach Montreux. Gstaad on the main route of course is full of banks, and Chateau d'Oex is well supplied.

Alternative route: Hahnenmoospass to Lenk via Pommernpass (4hr 30min)

The advantage of this alternative is a more varied and interesting descent that makes a visit to the fine Simmenfälle (waterfalls); the disadvantage being the extra 2hr 30min required for the walk above that of the main route. ▶

Only take this route if the weather is settled.

Instead of crossing the Hahnenmoospass, bear left and take a path leading round the hillside towards the lump of the **Regenboldshorn**. The way climbs to gain a fairly narrow but grassy pass to the west (right) of this peak. Unnamed on either the LS or K&F maps, this is the **Pommernpass** (2055m, **40min**). Given sufficient time and energy, the 15min ascent of the Regenboldshorn is worth making – turn left at the pass – for the views are particularly fine from the summit.

Descending from the pass the trail veers left and heads over steep pastures, passing haybarns and farms,

*Lenk is a fine walking
centre at the head
of the Simmental*

and then enters forest. At a junction of paths follow signs
for the Simmenfälle. These are reached about 2hr from
the Pommernpass.

> The snows of the Plaine Morte, and the Wildstrubel's
> northern glaciers, drain as a number of streams that
> combine to form the Simme, a river which gives its
> name to the Simmental. The Truebbach, Laubbach
> and Emmertenbach all come together below the
> Ammertenhorn as one riotous, foaming spout. The
> **Simmenfälle** are seen where they escape a rocky
> confine and are then channelled along a man-made
> gully through woods and down into the bed of the
> upper Simmental. It's a spectacular sight and worth
> a diversion to experience.

Do not cross the bridge at the top of the falls,
but descend a gravel track down to the Simmenfälle
Restaurant at **Oberreid** (1105m). From here an hourly bus
travels to Lenk, while the continuing walk by the signed
path will take a little over an hour. Take the riverside path,
cross the river after 500 metres and wander along a pleasant path all the way to **Lenk**.

STAGE 15
Lenk to Gstaad by the Trütlisbergpass

Start	Lenk 1064m
Finish	Gstaad 1050m
Distance	22.5km
Total ascent	1150m
Total descent	1160m
Time	7hr
High point(s)	Trütlisbergpass 2037m
Maps	LS 5009 Gstaad–Adelboden; K&F 32 Crans-Montana
Transport	Gondola (Lenk–Betelberg–Leiterli)
Accommodation	Gstaad – hotels, camping, B&B

This is an easy stage of high mountain walking. The Trütlisbergpass is straightforward and grassy, with a couple of outstanding viewpoints close by, although the col itself misses some of the best views. Take time out on the Tube, a tiny summit of 2106m but with panoramic views from Les Diablerets to the Eiger.

The descent to Gstaad (pronounced 'stardt' with a semi-silent 'g') is a long, pleasant walk following the Turbach river through pasture and woodland, with the path eventually dropping you in the centre of Gstaad and its ritzy shops (Prada is on the left, should you fancy such things, just after the Louis Vuitton outlet).

An alternative start is to take the Betelberg cable car to the Leiterli top station and contour to the Trütlisbergpass in 1hr 15min, passing fascinating limestone scenery and an interesting ridge through water-gouged runnels. If staying in a hotel in Lenk, request a visitors' card which gives free access to the lift.

From **Lenk** railway station cross the main road and continue slightly uphill on Rawilstrasse, past hotels and restaurants. When the road turns left, take Hohenliebe, straight ahead. The path climbs steep steps past chalets. After 8min turn right across pastures with fine views down to Lenk and back to Stage 14. Turn left on a road climbing alongside the Wallbach river, soon coming to a car park and small cable lift (**20min**). About 100 metres after this, turn right on a broad path. ▶

At the time of writing there are repairs in the gorge following storm damage, so check for diversions around the Wallbachschlucht.

Cross the river on a bridge, turn left, and then left again at the next two path junctions. Climb alongside the river on steps, ladders and walkways by the attractive waterfalls and bustling stream. After 45min you arrive quite unexpectedly at **Wallegg** (1327m).

Turn right uphill alongside a small ski piste, passing five carved wooden statues of the founders of the Betelsbahn cableway (used on the alternative ascent route – see below). The path climbs gradually and meets the stream again after 1hr 10min. After a steep climb on which roots act as steps, reach a track at 1548m and turn left.

The track continues the steady uphill progress until a right turn where a sign gives 1hr 30min to the pass (so far you've climbed 500m in **1hr 30min**). Pass a small stable and continue to climb (the hillside is potentially marshy and grazing cows soon make it very muddy), to reach a prominent farm building where you turn right onto a broader, occasionally muddy, track that continues to gain height. At one point the way becomes indistinct; here you follow the general line downhill (there may be a tiny tarn surrounded by reeds in wet

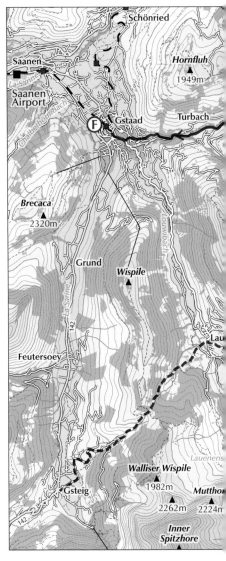

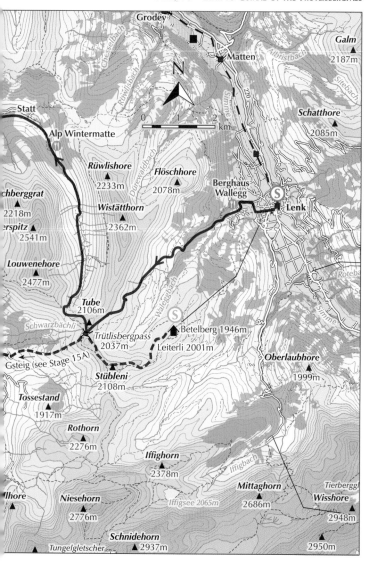

The cows in this region must have a surprisingly high level of intelligence, judging from the fiendish gates and electric fence crossings, which can be challenging for walkers.

weather). You can see the col about 100m higher, along a steadily climbing path. ◄

Reach the **Trütlisberg Pass** (2037m, **3hr 30min**) after almost 1000m of ascent. The views have been steadily expanding, but the best spots are around 400 metres further on or by climbing the **Tube** at 2106m. Although it barely deserves the term 'peaklet', it has dramatic 360-degree views; back to the Eiger and along the line of the Bernese Alps, with the Wildhorn the closest and most impressive, despite reaching only 3246m.

From the col the path turns sharp right and then curves to the left and drops down a ridge between the two valleys to reach Turli, a second col (1993m, **3hr 50min**). Views to the west include Lauenen (shown on the signpost as around 1hr 30min below), and across to Les Diablerets and the ongoing route (Stage 16).

Turn right at Turli to descend into the wide U-shaped valley, truly a classic example of the impact of glaciers. If you are feeling energetic, the Giferspitz offers an exciting afternoon's work, with even better views and an extra 500m of up and down, but also a direct descent into Gstaad.

Five minutes below the col, turn right at a farm building. Follow the path (not the higher traversing track) that heads downhill into the valley, indicated by marker posts. Descend over marshy ground protected by a metal walkway and stone steps, which continues for around 1km as the path drops down into scrubby bushes.

Around 25min from the col pass a small farm building (at this point look out for a path on the other side of the valley). A track joins from the left; continue downhill. At 40min pass a cableway crossing the Turbach river and running up the hillside across the valley. It's a very attractive spot, with the contrasts of bright green grass and dark green pines now visible in the views ahead. Wildflowers proliferate early in the year.

About 55min from the col at 1560m the path crosses the river, continuing on a good track on the east side of the valley. In 3min join the farm track you noted earlier on the other side of the valley. As the way gradually swings to the left, views back to the Trütlisberg Pass are lost. The track becomes concrete and descends more steeply through full-grown pines, the views ahead (if anything) improving. ▶

Even early in heavy-snow years, the valley is likely to be clear as it gets the full midday sun, despite facing north.

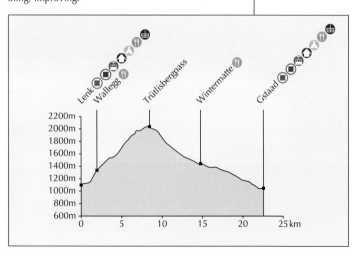

153

The long and wide Turbach valley on the way to Gstaad

After 15min come to the **Wintermatte** (bar restaurant, 1422m, 5hr 10min from Lenk, 1hr 30min from the Turli col). This makes a fine place for a break, perhaps lunch if you started early and made good progress, and is highly recommended.

Cross the river (just before the restaurant) and take the path along the opposite bank. The path recrosses the Turbach, then turns left by a shed and into trees along the river bank rather than climbing to the road. The wide track continues alongside the attractive stream, easy walking through mixed woodland.

Pass a picnic and play area at 1250m, soon after which you come to a road at a hairpin. Turn left along the road, with good views towards Les Diablerets. In another 5min the path climbs above the road, and 100 metres later turns left, climbing gently and traversing high above the river, with broadening views to the west.

The descent into Gstaad seems to be re-routed frequently due to building work. Look carefully for the infrequent signs lest you get distracted by the unaffordable chalets.

The way emerges at a barn and descends a meadow to the first chalets of Gstaad. Go down the road between villas, turn left then right, and then left again. ◄ Keep heading downhill and the route will clarify. Leave the road and keep to a descending path in woods past chalets and emerge at a road facing the railway, turn left and emerge in the centre of **Gstaad** (1050m, **7hr**).

GSTAAD (1050M)

Gstaad is a busy resort with all manner of shops and expensive hotels. Mainly chalets, very pricey and reputed to host the famous, it's a far cry from most of the small villages on the VA. Gstaad hosts one of the ritziest shopping streets in Switzerland and has an events schedule, both summer and winter, that rivals many cities.

Tourist information (tel 033 748 81 81, www.gstaad.ch). Hotels, shops, banks, post office, rail connections with Saanen, Zweisimmen, Bern and Geneva. Camping Bellerive, tel 033 744 63 30, www.bellerivecamping.ch, Hotel Bellerive tel 033 748 88 33, www.bellerive-gstaad.ch (both 1km north of town). Lower-priced accommodation includes Ferienhaus Alpenblick (tel 033 744 18 14, several B&Bs (the tourist office holds a list) and a youth hostel in nearby Saanen (tel 033 744 13 43, www.youthhostel.ch/gstaadsaanenland).

Alternative route – Lenk to the Trütlisberg Pass via Betelberg gondola (1hr 15min)

The Betelberg gondola station is located near the south-west outskirts of **Lenk**. The cableway rises in two stages and you disembark at Leiterli (1946m), the top station. Nearby is **Berghotel Leiterli** (beds and dormitory accommodation, refreshments, tel 033 736 30 00, www.huettenzauber.ch). At the time of writing Lenk hotels provide a visitor pass that gives access to the lift without charge, but this may change. ▶

On leaving the gondola station take a track (sign to Lauenen), which rounds the first hump to a little col where it then continues on the south side of the ridge. The direct route to Lauenen keeps on this side over the 1992m Stüblenepass, but a much more interesting (and not much longer) route forks right – take this path – signed to the Trütlisberg Pass. This cuts below the **Stübleni** peak above spiny limestone ribs at the head of the Wallbach valley, after which you climb to the rocky ridge, which gives an exciting tight-rope path among a mass of mini-craters. Pass a small shelter hut and descend left to the **Trütlisberg Pass** (2037m, 1hr 15min from Berghotel Leiterli).

From here you gain splendid grandstand views back to Hahnenmoos, and into the craggy combes of Wildhorn and Wildstrubel.

STAGE 16
Gstaad to L'Etivaz by the Col de Jable

Start	Gstaad 1050m
Finish	L'Etivaz 1140m
Distance	16.5km
Total ascent	1170m
Total descent	1080m
Time	6hr 30min
High point(s)	Col de Jable 1883m
Maps	LS 5009 Gstaad–Adelboden; K&F 32 Crans-Montana and 16 Gruyère
Transport	Trains, buses (from Gstaad); postbus (L'Etivaz–Col des Mosses and Chateau d'Oex). Cable car (Gstaad to Eggli)
Accommodation	L'Etivaz – hotel

Considering the size of Gstaad, escape is amazingly pain-free and you are well outside it within 10min. But the climb to Eggli is steep, through pastures and woodlands, then along a broad ridge among inoffensive ski-lifts and, much better, dairy farms, some of which serve drinks and food. The climb to the broad Col de Jable along the Trittlisattel is always interesting. From here on you need to switch to speaking French, for this is the linguistic divide. You may find more farms open for refreshments on the descent in high summer. Descending in steep forest, you will probably hear L'Etivaz before you see it. Allow some time here, especially if you are interested in cheese, as it is a major centre of mountain cheesemaking from the milk of the many herds in the region.

There is limited accommodation in L'Etivaz. Alternative accommodation options reached by bus are at La Lécherette, Col des Mosses and Chateau d'Oex. Strong walkers could combine this stage with Stage 17, walking as far as Chateau d'Oex.

From the centre of **Gstaad** head to the south end of the pedestrianised street and cross the bridge over the Louwibach. Turn right, slightly downhill, signed Col de

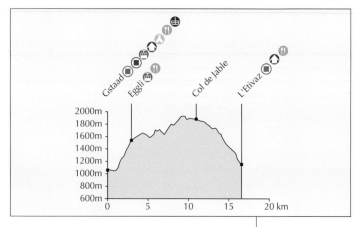

Jable and L'Etivaz, and walk out of town to a roundabout; go straight across. The town quickly ends and you pass the chalets of Rütti. The strangely shaped canvas roof of a sports complex is visible on the right. Cross a bridge and turn right, and you are in fields in less than 10min. (Left leads to the Eggli lift bottom station). Follow the track which looks to be headed uphill, but a sign takes you left around a house before climbing steeply up the side of fields and into woods.

The middle-mountain walking above Gstaad still has sharp peaks

Schönried

Hornfluh ▲ 1949m

Louwibach

Wispile ◄

Gstaad Ⓢ

Saanen

Grund

Eggli

142 La Sarine

11

Feutersoey

Chalberhornbach

Rougemont

Le Rubli ▲ 2285m

La Videmanette ▲ 2187m

Pointes de Sur Combe

Col de Jable 1883m

Furggenspiz ▲ 2297m

La Sarine

Wild Boden

▲ 2393m

Le Gummfluh ▲ 2458m

Wittenberghorn ▲ 2350m

Tschärzisbach

Laitemaire ▲ 1678m

La Gérine

Rocher du Midi ▲ 2096m

Le Biolet ▲ 2293m

Vanil Carré ▲ 2195m

Pointe de Cray ▲ 2070m

Château-d'Oex

La Yausseresse

Plan de la Douve 2170m

La Tornaresse

L'Etivaz Ⓕ

L'Eau Froide Pays d'Enhaut

Ruisseau des Méris

11

Rossinière

La Tornaresse

La Torneresse

de Cuites

11

N

0   1   2 km

From here on, it's all steep, steep and even steeper to the Eggli ski station. Climb through alternating woods and pastures, the wonderful shade of mixed beech woods gradually giving way to pine forest. Pass farms and cross roads, always heading up. Eventually the path joins a grassed ski slope and you will see the **Eggli** ski station buildings above, which you reach in 1hr 40min from Gstaad, after a climb of 500m.

At 1557m there's a restaurant (Berggasthaus Eggli) at the lift station with fine views south to the Wildhorn and Gsteig.

The trail descends to the right of the ski station before coming to a path junction, where you continue straight on. Soon rejoining one of the ski access tracks, climb past a higher ski-lift station and a barn with a welcome water supply. It becomes apparent you are on a broad ridge headed directly towards the Col de Jable, which can be clearly seen ahead. Pass the Vorders Eggli farm (1660m, **2hr**, refreshments) and continue along the ridge, losing 80m of hard-earned height to a broad saddle, before climbing again through pasture and into woodland (signed **Wild Boden**). The path keeps to the north of the ridge, traversing among trees, sometimes sloping steeply through the wood (which, as the name suggests, is rather wild). After 1.5km descend again to another saddle with a dairy farm (Wilde Bode 1645m, **2hr 45min**). ▸

There are dramatic views ahead to the limestone cliffs of the 2458m Gummfluh.

(If you are pushed for time, or tiring after two weeks on trek, the good farm road straight ahead leads to the Col de Jable in about 45min – about half the time needed on the signed Trüttlisattel path, although taking it would miss all the fun of this minor spur of the Gummfluh.)

Take the path to the right here and climb steeply through more woods, partly felled, to the Trittlisattel, with fine views south and east. The path climbs then undulates among woodland and limestone outcrops and crosses screes, with a short section through a defile before traversing the hillside on the way to the Col de Jable.

The best views are to be had before reaching the col, which is slightly lower than the traversing path, so you descend to it. From the **Col de Jable** (1883m, **4hr 45min**),

Approaching the Gummfluh along the Trittlisattel ridge

signed 1hr 45min to L'Etivaz, views to the west are of steadily lower hills.

From the col take the higher, well-signed path to the right. It traverses the hillside through high dairy pastures, passing farms along the way, at the first of which (15min from the col) you may find refreshments in high summer. The route continues, sometimes path, sometimes track, occasionally muddy and dropping into forest at a gate. Starting to descend steeply, take two right turns, signed *'sentier'* (50min from the col) rather than *'route'*. The forest is mainly pine, with glimpses of the pastures and valley below. Drop directly into the village, which you approach through pastures, and then a signed path that takes a cunning route between houses and past the church, before bringing you to the Hotel du Chamois, the village bus stop and *cave à fromage* – a substantial cheese factory in **L'Etivaz** (1140m, **6hr 30min**).

L'ETIVAZ (1140M)

Situated midway along the route linking Château d'Oex and Col des Mosses, and famed for the hard cheese made locally, the tiny village of L'Etivaz has a population of less than 200 which swells to several thousand for the annual 1 October festival for the cows being taken to lower pastures and indoors.

B&B accommodation in L'Etivaz, with restaurant, is at the rustic Hotel du Chamois (tel 026 924 62 66, www.hotelduchamois.ch), open daily in summer but closed part of the week from end of August (check with facility for details). Off route facilities in Col des Mosses and hotels 2hr 30min walk further in Château d'Oex (see Stage 18). If you need to transfer to Château d'Oex by public transport, buses leave hourly until around 19:00 taking 25min.

See introductory notes at the beginning of this stage for ways to extend the day's route if required. It is also possible to take a direct route to the Col de Sonlomont from L'Etivaz (see Direct route alternative in Stage 17), thereby omitting Stage 17 and saving a day's walk.

L'Etivaz is surrounded by green pasture, even at the end of the summer

STAGE 17
L'Etivaz to Rossinière

Start	L'Etivaz 1140m
Finish	Rossinière 918m
Distance	14.5km
Total ascent	300m
Total descent	520m
Time	4hr
High point(s)	L'Etivaz 1140m
Maps	LS 262T Rochers de Naye; K&F 16 Gruyère
Transport	Bus (L'Etivaz–Chateau d'Oex), train (Chateau d'Oex to Rossinière and ultimately Montreux)
Accommodation	Chateau d'Oex – hotels, youth hostel; and Rossinière – hotel, guesthouse

This is a transitional stage through lower countryside to position the trekker at Rossinière for the start of the long stage to Rochers de Naye. As such it's quite different in character from the mountain stages just completed but continues the trend of steadily lower and gentler stages as Montreux is approached. It could be combined with the previous stage to L'Etivaz, perhaps with some assistance from the postbus.

The stage begins with a walk down alongside the Torneresse river before climbing a little above the cliffs of the Pissot gorge and crossing farmland before taking in the Pont de Turrian suspension bridge and climbing into the long-established cheese-making centre of Chateau d'Oex (pronounced 'day'). The onward route to Rossinière crosses fields and the La Sarine river (twice) before entering the village.

For trekkers wanting to omit Stage 17, this turn provides a route to the Col de Sonlomont – see Direct route below.

From the centre of **L'Etivaz**, head down below the Maison De L'Etivaz and alongside the river. Continue through pastures and past a farm before entering woodlands where the route is both delineated and protected by a series of boardwalks (protected by wire mesh and so not slippery). At the Torrent des Ciernes Raynaud, pass the left turn to Col des Mosses and keep right on a good track. ◄ Cross the river and soon emerge at the road (**1hr**).

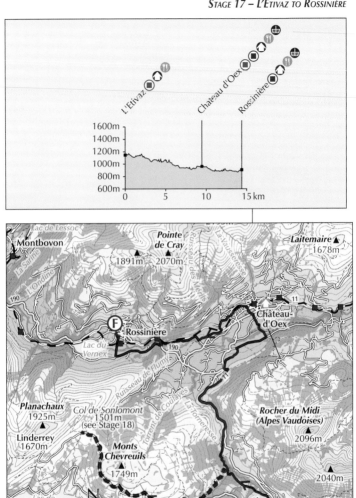

163

The Hotel du Chamois in L'Etivaz, a genuine original

Direct route from L'Etivaz to the Col de Sonlomont

By taking a direct line from L'Etivaz to the Col de Sonlomont, it is possible to save a day of walking at the price of a 30min extension to Stage 18's walk to Rochers de Naye.

At the Torrent des Ciernes Raynaud (**35min**), turn left uphill, initially in pastures and then in woods. After a climb of about 1km, meet a road near a hairpin and continue uphill to **La Lécherette** (1379m, **1hr 35min**). Turn up through the village, taking a path between houses and come to a narrow road. Turn left and follow this road to the **Col de Sonlomont** (1501m, **3hr**). It is also possible to take a bus from L'Etivaz to La Lécherette. From the Col continue on the route in Stage 18.

Official route continues

Continue down the road for 2min and take the path on the right that climbs above the road. The Gorge du Pissot's cliffs can be seen below. The path turns a corner at Les Montees and descends to meet a road at La Rosettaz. Follow the path as it makes its way through pastures before coming to a quiet road. Turn right along this and come to a left turn (the second left turn is best) and drop down on a good path to the Pont Turrian. ◄

The bridge is the oldest suspension bridge in French-speaking Switzerland, originally built in 1883.

Cross the only slightly wobbly bridge and climb zigzags then quiet lanes before crossing the busy D11 to reach the central square of **Chateau d'Oex** with the Hotel de Ville (in Switzerland a *hotel de ville* is actually a hotel, unlike in France) on the right (958m, **2hr 30min**).

The gentle hills around La Lécherette on the alternative route to the Col de Sonlomont

CHATEAU D'OEX (958M)

A small town, often twinned with Rougemont higher up the valley, Chateau d'Oex continues with the tradition of cheesemaking seen in L'Etivaz but is also a small resort and has become a centre of hot air ballooning. It has road links to Col des Mosses and Lac Léman and rail links direct to both Gstaad and Montreux.

Facilities include hotels, restaurants, pharmacy, trains, buses and food shops. Accommodation includes Hôtel Roc et Neige (tel 026 924 33 59, www.roc-et-neige.ch); Hotel de Ville (tel 026 924 74 77, www.hdvoex.ch); Hotel du Gare (tel 026 924 77 17 www.buffet-doex.ch); youth hostel (tel 026 924 64 04, www.youthhostel.ch).

To continue the route, head straight ahead upwards from the central plaza, and turn left at the railway tracks. Follow the route past sports facilities and past chalets of the La Frasse suburb before making a decisive turn left through farmland. Continue down and cross the railway line (with

Looking across the Sarine river to the quiet village of Rossinière, home to Switzerland's largest wooden building

two trains per hour it's safe to cross). Approach the road at Le Pré d'En Haut but keep right at the last minute and descend to a junction where you turn right on a track.

Climb alongside the river before dropping down to the Pont de la Chaudenne; turn left on the road across the bridge and then right on a minor road, pass a recycling centre and enjoy the lane as it crosses farmland and Rossinière comes into view. Turn right (tomorrow's onward route turns left here), drop down to cross the Sarine river and climb into **Rossinière** (918m, **4hr**).

ROSSINIÈRE (918M)

Only an hour's walk from Chateau d'Oex, Rossinière is a quiet village along the rail line to Montreux and makes a good start point for the longer day to Rochers de Naye. It is also home to the Grand Chalet, Switzerland's largest habitable wooden house, but it is not possible to visit.

Facilities include hotels, B&B, food shops. Accommodation at B&B Chalet La Pivoine (tel 079 305 52 67, www.bb-la-pivoine.vaudhotels.com), Hotel de Ville (tel 026 924 65 40, www.hotel-rossiniere.ch); Elite (tel 026 924 52 12, www. restaurant-elite.vaudhotels.com).

STAGE 18

Rossinière to Rochers de Naye
by the Col de Sonlomont

Start	Rossinière 918m
Finish	Rochers de Naye 1971m
Distance	19km
Total ascent	1900m
Total descent	850m
Time	8hr
High point(s)	Rochers de Naye 1971m
Maps	LS 262T Rochers de Naye; K&F 16 Gruyère
Transport	Train (Rossinière to Allières, and ultimately Montreux)
Accommodation	Col des Mosses – hotel (off route); Rochers de Naye – hotel with dormitory and yurts; Sonchaux (1hr 15min beyond Rochers de Naye) – auberge with dormitories

Although the trek is drawing to a close, the walking remains of a high standard. Lac de l'Hongrin provides interest, while the broader views to hills not seen before are enticing. From Rossinière, the trail climbs a potentially difficult and exposed hillside path (Les Traverses) to get to the Col de Sonlomont. Unfortunately all the height gained is lost in a steep descent to La Vuichoude d'en Bas, then regained en route to the Col de Chaude before the ridge route to Rochers de Naye.

If desired, Les Traverses can be avoided by train or bus to different start points, while if there is high wind or stormy conditions as you approach the Rochers, a direct descent from the Col de Chaude is more secure. There is yurt and other accommodation at Rochers de Naye, and accommodation possibilities on the descent route to Montreux.

A direct route from L'Etivaz to the Col de Sonlomont is described in Stage 17 (see above), and the route from Col des Mosses (on the alternative routing) is described in Stage 16A.

From the centre of **Rossinière**, head downhill past the station, cross the river and go straight ahead at the path junction. Cross pastures and climb into woods.

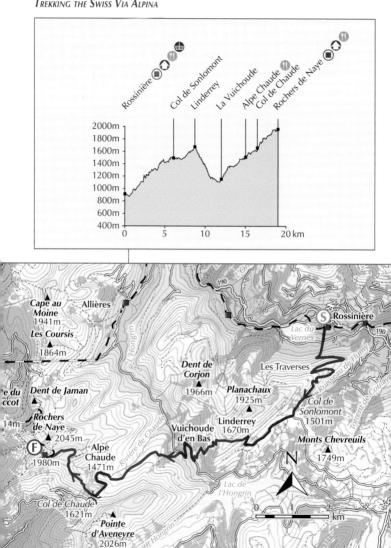

On the map the path climbs in gentle loops up the 400m wooded hillside. On the ground, however, while the angle of climb up **Les Traverses** is reasonable, the walking conditions are potentially challenging. The hillside is very steep and there are significant drop-offs in many places. In good weather it's an exposed but reasonable and, for some, a challenging proposition. In wet weather, it's quite different, with wet leaves, slippery mud, roots and rocks all vying to cause a misstep. The second major zag to the south has sections partially protected by cables. If you are affected by exposure, it may be better to take a different route under these conditions.

By the end of the second (southward zag), the difficulties are largely over. Emerge into pastures and pass the isolated farm at La Tanchin (1301m). Climb a broad ridge and after an abandoned building take a pleasant track that becomes a path before joining a track to climb to the **Col de Sonlomont** (1501m, **2hr 30min** under good conditions and 3hr or more under poor conditions). ▶

The connecting routes from L'Etivaz (see Stage 17) and Col des Mosses (see Stage 16A) join the main route here.

The Lac de l'Hongrin and its barrage

Options to avoid Les Traverses

There are various public transport options available in Rossinière to avoid the ascent of Les Traverses:

- **Train and bus to La Lécherette** and take the paved farm lane for the Col de Sonlomont.
- **Train to Allières** and walk up the quiet road to La Vuichaude d'en Bas and continue the climb to the Col de Chaude. See notes in the stage introduction on planning for the last few stages.

Main route

Turn right and continue on farm roads. After 30min the route starts to climb the flanks of Planachaux, before the road turns rapidly to track, then path, and climbs to **Linderrey** (1670m). Here you get views across to the Col de Chaude and Rochers de Naye, which a crow would reach in less than four level kilometres, but the walker has to descend over 500m before climbing to regain them.

Alpe Chaude, possible refreshments before the final climb to the Rochers de Naye

Drop steeply down the hillside, looking for marker posts in the fields; early on the path is very vague. Descend past a prominent farm and continue on switchbacks all the way to the road at 1201m. Turn right and follow the road through two large zigzags and come out at the farm of **La Vuichoude d'en Bas** (1103m, **4hr 30min**). Turn left and

climb through fields and into woods. Here you may meet barbed-wire gates that present a real challenge. Climb again in open fields past a farm building (Vuichoude d'en Haut (1341m)). The path contours south-west around the hillside before entering boggy woodland.

Climb to **Alp Chaude** (1471m, refreshments), from where the route continues up the farm road to reach the **Col de Chaude** (1621m, **6hr 30min**). This provides your first view of Lac Léman, and the mountains to its south and east. ▶

Turn right up the steep path signed for Rochers de Naye. Climbing steeply, at first through woods, then over grass slopes, the path emerges onto a fairly sharp grassy crest that requires a little care, before dropping to Plan d'Areine (1874m) and a solitary building. The way then climbs a traversing route, then over a crest from where the **Rochers de Naye** hotel and railway are clearly visible. The path climbs again to the Jardin Alpin before dropping to the pass (1971m), and in a few more metres, the Grand Hotel (**8hr**).

The ridge between the Col de Chaude and the Rochers de Naye

If conditions are poor, the ridge may be unviable so consider a descent from the Col de Chaude – follow tracks to Sonchaux and join the VA route to Montreux.

ROCHERS DE NAYE (1971M)

This is one of the classic viewpoints enjoyed by visitors to Montreux, who ride to the summit on one of Switzerland's famous cog railways. Lac Léman lies 1500m below.

Botanical garden, two restaurants, hotel with standard beds, dormitories and yurts (bookable through accommodation apps).

STAGE 19
Rochers de Naye to Montreux

Start	Rochers de Naye 1971m
Finish	Montreux 370m
Distance	14km
Total ascent	50m
Total descent	1650m
Time	4hr
High point(s)	Rochers de Naye 1971m
Maps	LS 262T Rochers de Naye; K&F 16 Gruyère
Transport	Train from Rochers de Naye to Montreux, stops in Caux and Glion
Accommodation	Sonchaux – auberge with dormitories; Caux – hotel; Glion – hotel; Montreux – hotels, pensions, youth hostel

The final day of the VA is a long and in places spectacular downhill trek. Unless prevented by lack of time or bad weather, this is definitely the way to finish. The first few hundred metres are down a long ridge directly from the Rochers de Naye with views to the east and south. An old track has been restored to a high standard providing this unique finalé. Later, after Glion, the route descends its final few hundred metres down the Gorge de Chauderon, a world apart from the VA and indeed from Montreux. It's almost a scene from the set of Jurassic Park (without the dinosaurs), emerging close to the centre of Montreux.

Note that the Gorge de Chauderon is subject to flooding and repairs and there may be diversions, so keep a look out.

Whether you were able to stay at the Rochers de Naye, in Montreux or perhaps the superbly placed Auberge de Sonchaux, this makes a fitting final day before taking a well-deserved lunch on the lake shore in Montreux, and either heading home or staying on to enjoy a post-trek rest.

Descend from the sign at the col, looping through a rather unexpected bridge under the path. Any fears that the route is going to be exposed, as might be surmised from a glance

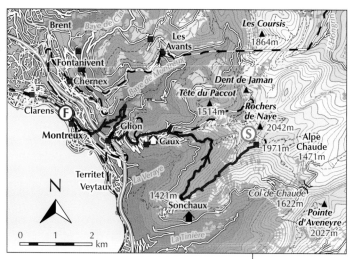

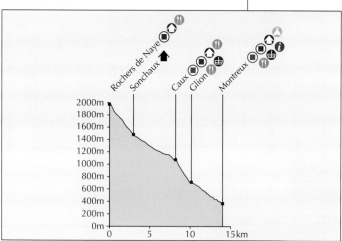

at the map, are quickly allayed as it becomes clear that the path is well made and descends at a relaxed pace. Initially (as for much of the descent) that path hugs the south side

A well-protected narrow path descends the ridge from the Rochers de Naye

of the long ridge, with views across to the Leysin tors and peaks across the Rhône, which is visible far below.

At 1832m reach a gap in the ridge with colossal views to the west, and the small cottage of Alp Sautodoz just off route. After a suitable photographic break, resume the descent. The path drops among forest and small cliffs; it is wide and well protected by new barriers for most of the descent to the farm at Creux à la Cierge, (1454m, **1hr**). From here it becomes a track descending through woodland to a viewpoint 15min later (benches, picnic hut, toilet).

> The **Sonchaux auberge** (1hr 15min) is a 150m and 15min descent (and 20min re-ascent) to the left, with remarkable views over the lake and the mountains to the south. Open May–October – not Tuesday except during July and August; dormitory accommodation and refreshments (tel 021 963 44 67, www.aubergedesonchaux.ch).

The auberge at Sonchaux, 15 minutes off route

From the picnic spot, descend to the north. The trail makes a long loop on a good and none-too-steep track. Pass a chalet 30min after the viewpoint (possible refreshments) and continue down. The way runs onto a road, and – just after crossing under a bridge carrying the railway line from Montreux to Rochers de Naye – you come out

Morning view across Lac Léman to the mountains south of the lake

at **Caux** (1048m, **2hr**, buses, rail station, post office, toilets, possible refreshments. Accommodation at Le CouCou (tel 021 961 25 91, www.coucoumontreux.com)).

The route continues down the road for 2min before turning sharply left on a steep and narrow path; this will carry you all the way to Glion, with but a single change in direction. Ignoring all distractions, it crosses the road many times, the railway once, and takes a direct line between houses and woods, before dropping into **Glion** (718m, **2hr 45min**) where the signs become a little intermittent.

> **Glion** Refreshments and full range of shops can be found in this eyrie of a village; funicular down to Montreux to save the last 45min of knee-crunching descent.

At an unmarked junction at the bottom of a long flight of steps, follow the road down and round to the right. Pass along the road in front of the hotel spotted a little earlier, and after 3min find a poorly marked left-hand turn. Take this and find signs at the bottom of a set of steps. Heading down, the road becomes a track passing a solitary house where you go straight ahead on a

path, then pass the fine-looking Restaurant de Chauderon before starting to descend steeply again into the Gorge de Chauderon. Cross the stream and turn left (it is well signed), and descend the gorge on a walkway. The route here is graded as a mountain path, and is well protected as it descends between cliffs. ▶

Pass under the motorway, which is carried by an elevated bridge, then climb briefly and pass an old factory with a large chimney before entering old **Montreux** (hotels, refreshments, buses, railway station) on narrow lanes, coming out by a bridge over the River Baye. The path continues to be marked and takes a direct diagonal descending line into the centre of town, passing a music conservatoire, school and crossing roads, before coming out at Montreux station.

Not far to go now: drop down through the station and into the streets below. Descend a long flight of steps, cross the main road and come out to the final VA signpost on the lake-shore promenade (374m, **4hr**).

Dipping your boots in the lake is not straightforward due to the shore protection, but perhaps dipping poles will be sufficient. The lake ferry is a short way to the left, should you feel you have the energy and another four weeks to contemplate continuing on to Nice down the GR5.

Congratulations – you have made it across Switzerland!

Vegetation and mossy streams tumble from high above, so the gorge has a tropical feel.

The end on the placid shore of the lake

MONTREUX (370M)

Situated on the south-east shore of Lac Léman, Montreux has been a noted resort for two hundred years and more. It was on the itinerary of many European travellers undertaking the Grand Tour during the 18th and 19th centuries, the medieval Château de Chillon being the main attraction. Byron (whose *Prisoner of Chillon* is one of his most oft-quoted works), Shelley, Dumas, Flaubert, Hugo and Dickens all came here, but long before their time the site of the castle was occupied in the Bronze Age, and later by the Romans. In more recent times, the two-week Montreux Jazz Festival takes place every July. Freddie Mercury of Queen is celebrated as well.

Much of the modern town is rather less attractive than its setting, however, for like so many European cities it has a surfeit of high-rise blocks that seem sorely out of place. Yet its position on the lakeside is its most forgiving and endearing feature. A lakeside walk to the castle among exquisite gardens, with the impressive Dents du Midi as a backdrop, is highly recommended.

Tourist information (tel 084 886 84 84, www.montreuxriviera.com). Hotels, pensions, youth hostel, restaurants, shops, banks, post office; rail links with Geneva, and (change at Lausanne) Zürich; lake ferry to Geneva etc. There is a wide selection of accommodation at all prices, Some lower-priced accommodation: youth hostel (tel 021 963 49 34, www.youthhostel.ch/montreux), Hotel Élite (tel 021 966 03 03), Hotel La Rouvenaz (tel 021 963 27 36, www.rouvenaz.ch), Pension-Villa Germaine (tel 021 963 15 28), B&B Belalp (tel 079 213 85 56, www.bnb-belalp.ch).

RETURNING HOME

Assuming you have tickets for a flight home, you will need to reach either Geneva or Zürich airports. For the former, regular direct trains leave Montreux railway station about once an hour, while for Zürich you will need to change in Lausanne. The Montreux-to-Geneva route is a very scenic one as it traces the shoreline of Lac Léman virtually all the way. However, for a more leisurely (and romantic) journey, you might like to consider the lake ferry which takes about 5hr, including stops, to reach Geneva from Montreux.

ALTERNATIVE ROUTE
AFTER LENK

STAGE 15A
Lenk to Gsteig by the Trütlisbergpass

Start	Lenk 1064m
Finish	Gsteig 1183m
Distance	22.5km
Total ascent	1500m
Total descent	1380m
Time	8hr
High point(s)	Trütlisberg Pass 2037m; Krinnen Pass 1660m
Maps	LS 5009 Gstaad–Adelboden; K&F 32 Crans Montana
Transport	Gondola (Lenk–Betelberg–Leiterli)
Accommodation	Berghotel Leiterli (via gondola); Lauenen (5hr 20min) – hotels; Gsteig – hotels, camping

Despite its length, and the fact that there are two passes to cross, this most enjoyable stage does not seem as demanding as the statistics might indicate. It leads across a transverse ridge that has pastureland to its very crest; a limestone landscape, rucked and pitted but extravagant with flowers during the early summer. The Trütlisberg Pass is just far enough away from the main range of Oberland peaks to provide a vast, sweeping panorama. Then, beyond Lauenen, the wooded Krinnen Pass (or Chrinepass on some maps, or just Chrine) presents you with a vista dominated by the bold massif of Les Diablerets. Between these two passes, Lauenen sinks into a lush valley below the Wildhorn, while Gsteig nestles at the foot of Col du Pillon, the road pass which marks the western limit of the Bernese Alps. Both Lauenen and Gsteig have much to commend them. They're small, neat and pretty villages, bright with window boxes and with well-stocked food stores, modest hotels and, of course, opportunities for refreshment.

On this stage you begin to sense that the trek is drawing to a close, for this is a part of Switzerland mostly bypassed by tourist hype. But if you imagined that the magic would fade when your back was turned to the

Jungfrau, the final two or three days will surely prove you wrong. Should you feel the need for an easier morning, the Betelberg/Leiterli gondola is worth considering. It cuts at least 2hr from the walking time, saves almost 900m of height gain, and presents you with an entertaining alternative route to the Trütlisberg Pass. This is described below.

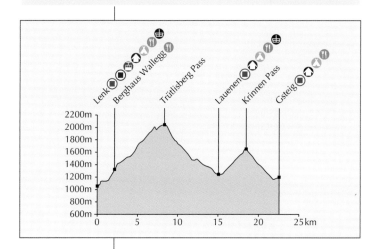

From the tourist information office in the heart of **Lenk**, walk up the main street a short distance towards the church, and go straight ahead on Hohenlieb when the road makes a left-hand turn. Ascend steps between chalets, then turn right and north to the Wallegg road and follow this alongside the **Wallbach** stream until just after passing a chairlift – where the road curves left – go ahead on a broad path/track into woods. The path climbs steeply. You then ascend a series of steel ladders and stone steps with water-falls thundering to one side among chasms of scoured and polished rocks of the Wallbachschlucht. At the top of these steps the way crosses to the left and resumes uphill.

About 1hr after leaving Lenk you emerge from the woods to a steep grassy clearing a little above Berghaus Wallegg (1327m, refreshments). Turn right and walk up

the right-hand side of the sloping meadow for about 100 metres, where you take a track into the woods again. This makes an easy contour, then gains a little height before crossing the Wallbach once more, shortly after which you leave the woods on an enclosed footpath leading to a farm track where you turn left. (There are good views from here towards the Hahnenmoos back in the east.)

A few paces after crossing a streambed, break to the right on a path which climbs a rough hillside – this can be extremely muddy following wet weather – and pass several farm buildings, the last of which is Ober Lochberg (1910m, **3hr**). All the way to the pass now views to the left are delightful, where the larger snow peaks rim the horizon, and the middle ground consists of one folding ridge after another – a grassy corrugation edged with the dark outline of forest strips. ▶

The first of these intermediate ridges carries the Betelberg gondola.

Just beyond the Ober Lochberg farm the way forks. Take the left branch across a stream, then continue up towards the Trütlisberg saddle, passing a small hut on the way. At last, you gain the **Trütlisberg Pass** (2037m, **3hr 30min**) which is marked by a signpost at a path junction.

A DIFFERENT CROSSING EVERY TIME

The first time I came onto this pass, two of us sat in the bright August sunshine waiting for a group that never arrived. We idled among the flowers, gazed at hawks hovering above us, at distant mountains we attempted to name. We scanned each valley and each individual ridge through binoculars, and wondered about the limestone pits around us. We listened to the insects, the low brush of a breeze among heavy-headed grasses, and the hollow hum of distance which only the deaf or ignorant call silence. Nearly two hours ticked by and the group failed to show, but in the peace and the sunshine I thought I'd found heaven. A year later I gained the pass hunched in windproofs. There was a distinct taste of winter in the air, clouds were heavy and brooding and threatened snow. It was far too cold to linger, so after a brief pause, my companions and I set off again into the teeth of the wind. If nothing else, this illustrates the truth that every crossing of the VA provides a different range of experience.

From the pass bear left to follow a slightly rising path to another junction, then begin the descent proper by dropping down to the right on a trail (indistinct in places) which eases over pastures to the farm buildings of **Vordere Trütlisberg** (1818m). Here you come onto a farm track leading to a metalled road. Follow this down in lazy loops. Find a left turn onto a small track and follow this down through woods, pastures and farm buildings, occasionally touching and then leaving the road. A right turn (not well signed) descends in woodland alongside a stream, before slipping into **Lauenen** (**5hr 20min**) near the Hotel Wildhorn.

LAUENEN (1241M)

Though only a small, modest resort, Lauenen makes a commendable base for a few days of a walking holiday, with a number of fine outings on its doorstep. One of the best leads past the lovely Geltenschuss waterfall and up to the Gelten Hut set below the glaciers of the Wildhorn massif, while others entice walkers over various passes in the walling ridges of the Lauenental. South of the village the Lauenensee is an attractive shallow tarn on the edge of woodland.

Tourist information (tel 033 765 91 81, www.gstaad.ch). Hotels, B&B, shops, post office, bus link with Gstaad. Accommodation at: Hotel Wildhorn (tel 033 765 30 12, www.wildhorn. ch), and Hotel Alpenland (tel 033 765 55 66, www.alpenland.ch).

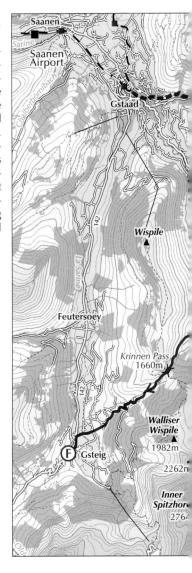

fluh
m

Schatthore
2085m

Rüwlishore
2228m

Flöschhore
2079m

Berghaus Wallegg

S *Lenk*

Giferspitz
2541m

Wistätthorn
2362m

Lauenenhore
2477m

to Gstaad
(see Stage 15)

Tube
2106m

Trütlisberg Pass
~2037m

S *Betelberg*
1946m

Leiterli
2001m

Lauenen

Vordere Trütlisberg

Oberlaubhore
1998m

Stübleni
2108m

Tossestand
1917m

N

0   1   2
km

Rothorn
2276m

Iffighorn
2378m

Mittaghorn
2686m

uenensee

utthore
2312m

Follhore

Niesehorn
2776m

Iffigsee 2065m

Rohrbachstein
2950m

Schnidehorn
2937m

Sex des Molettes
2782m

2819m

Tungelgletscher
2949m

Looking down onto gentler hills from above Lauenen

Turn left and walk along the main street towards the head of the Lauenental where the Wildhorn spreads a snowy mantle above a hanging valley. About 400 metres south of the village a signpost on the right of the road indicates the start of the path to the Krinnen Pass (Chrine) and Gsteig. Descend to a footbridge and cross the **Louwibach** stream. Over this go up to a farm road which snakes uphill past several houses, then take a path heading left uphill. This rises over meadows and alongside trees on the way to Sattel (1421m) near the top of a ski-tow. Follow a track over a stream, then onto the continuing path which climbs through woodland (where path construction has only partly tamed the boggy ground), and a little under 1hr 30min after leaving Lauenen you arrive at a little gap in a wooded ridge.

This is the **Krinnen Pass** (1660m, **6hr 50min**). Directly ahead you gaze into the upper Saanental, overlooked by the sprawling limestone massif of Les Diablerets, with the broad saddle of Col du Pillon below it to the right.

KRINNEN PASS

The Krinnen Pass, also known as the Chrinepass, is neither saddle nor col but a minor gap of 1659m in the wooded ridge that separates the Lauenental from the upper valley of the Saane. The pass is a useful crossing point from one valley to the other, but the ridge through which it cuts offers several very fine viewpoints and opportunities for day-walks of immense appeal. The ridge heading north (the Höhi Wispile), for example, has a path that traces its crest above the treeline before dropping at its far end to Gstaad. The southern extension of the ridge (the Walliser Wispile), however, leads to a rugged crest that climbs eventually to the 3036m Arpelistock which neighbours the Wildhorn. A short distance along that ridge, above the Krinnen Pass, there's a terrific viewpoint, and an alternative trail that descends to Gsteig via the alp of Vordere Wispile.

About 150m below the pass come to a farm whose track leads to a narrow road. Follow this downhill through a little valley, taking obvious footpath short cuts over meadows and through woods. About 30min or so from the pass, a path signed to Gsteig sends a route to the left, descending beside a stream before rejoining the road. Keep with this now, passing several chalets before coming onto the main Col du Pillon road near Hotel Viktoria. Turn left and walk into the small village of **Gsteig** (1183m, **8hr**).

GSTEIG (1183M)

Even smaller than Lauenen, Gsteig would also make a first-rate base for a walking holiday. With the limestone block of Les Diablerets looming from the south-west, one's attention is naturally focused there, but there are many other possibilities for active days out, whether walking or making the ascent of one or more of the neighbouring peaks. The village has none of the trappings of the larger Oberland resorts, but it has many very attractive buildings. Perhaps the best of these is the wonderful timber-built Hotel Bären (dating from 1756), with its richly decorated gables and flower-bright windows, which stands in the main street close to the 15th-century church. South of the village, at the head of a hanging valley between the Arpelistock and a spur of Mont Brun, the 2251m Col du Sanetsch is an old pass historically used for crossing from the Oberland to the Valais.

Tourist information (tel 033 748 81 81, www.gstaad.ch). Hotels, camping, restaurants, shop, post office, bus links with Gstaad and Les Diablerets. Accommodation at: Hotel Bären (tel 033 755 10 33, www.bären-gsteig.ch), Hotel Viktoria (tel 033 076 217 00 38), and Hotel-Restaurant Heiti (tel 033 755 11 54, www.restaurant-heiti.ch).

Alternative route: Lenk to the Trütlisbergpass via Betelberg gondola (1hr 15min)

The Betelberg gondola station is located near the south-west outskirts of **Lenk**. The cableway rises in two stages and you disembark at Leiterli (1946m), the top station. Nearby is Berghotel Leiterli (beds and dormitory accommodation, refreshments, tel 033 736 30 00, www.huettenzauber.ch). From here you gain splendid grand-stand views back to Hahnenmoos, and into the craggy combes of Wildhorn and Wildstrubel.

On leaving the gondola station take a track (sign to Lauenen), which rounds the first hump to a little col where it then continues on the south side of the ridge. The direct route to Lauenen keeps on this side over the 1992m Stüblenepass, but a much more interesting (and not much longer) route forks right – take this path – signed to the Trütlisberg Pass. This cuts below the **Stübleni** peak above spiny limestone ribs at the head of the Wallbach valley, after which you mount easily to the rocky ridge, an exciting tight-rope path among a mass of mini-craters.

The eroded limestone ribs above Leiterli

Pass a small shelter hut and descend left to the **Trütlisberg Pass** (2037m, about 1hr 15min from Leiterli.)

STAGE 16A

*Gsteig to Col des Mosses by
the Col des Andérets*

Start	Gsteig 1183m
Finish	Col des Mosses 1439m
Distance	25km
Total ascent	1470m
Total descent	1210m
Time	8hr
High point(s)	Blattipass 1918m; Col des Andérets 2030m
Maps	LS 5009 Gstaad-Adelboden; K&F 16 Gruyère and 32 Crans-Montana
Transport	Postbus, train (Gsteig–Les Diablerets–Montreux)
Accommodation	La Marnech/Isenau (4hr 45min) – restaurant with beds and dormitory accommodation; Col des Mosses – hotels with dormitory accommodation

This long, penultimate day's trek is both varied and visually rewarding from start to finish, for the landscape unfolds as you wander for hour after hour with an ever-changing panorama to enjoy. The Blattipass is one of the best viewpoints of the whole walk, revealing almost the complete line of the Bernese Oberland, including Wetterhorn, Eiger and wave upon wave of snowpeaks stretching as far as the slabs and glacial tongues of Les Diablerets.

After the Blattipass you plunge into a great vegetated basin with the Arnensee lake glistening in its hollow. Climbing out again you reach Col de Voré with a direct view of Les Diablerets, then wander round to Col des Andérets (more superb views) giving access to a new valley system, the first in canton Vaud. For more than 3hr you wander from alp to alp with a magical panorama that features (among others) the Dents du Midi and distant Mont Blanc. At Chersaule you make a traverse round the end of a long ridge below Pic Chaussy, and just short of the Oudiou alp, begin a forest and meadow walk leading into the valley of La Raverette – in French-speaking country now – and down to the little resort of Col des Mosses.

For walkers headed directly to the Rochers de Naye the next day, bypassing Chateau d'Oex and Rossinière, the section from Col des Mosses to the Col de Sonlomont is described.

From the centre of **Gsteig**, head back (north) towards Hotel Viktoria. Before reaching it take a narrow road signed Vorder Wallig, Arnensee, Seeberg and Col du Pillon. Passing several houses and farms, in 7min you turn right on another narrow road which soon becomes a track rising round the steeply wooded hillside. A few metres before the track comes to a farm building, take a path on the left and climb a very steep meadow edged with trees. Above this the way goes through a dense

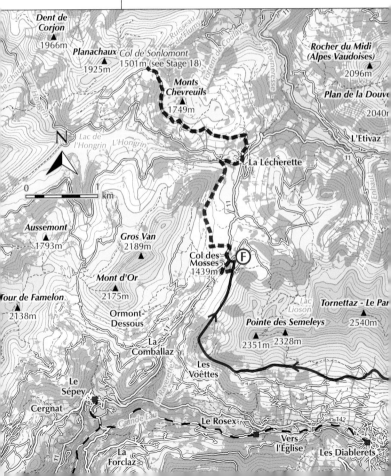

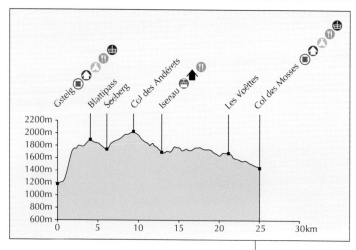

jungle of wild raspberries and into a grove of fir trees with views of Les Diablerets and below to Gsteig.

A large mountain massif carrying the canton boundaries of Bern and Vaud, **Les Diablerets** has a number of summits, the highest being 3216m. On the northern side it's strung about with cableways.

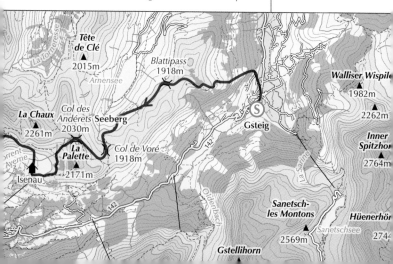

*Early morning climb
out of Gsteig*

It's one of the most
surprising and scenic
passes of the whole
route, and if you're
blessed with clear
visibility, you'll need
time to absorb it.

Les Diablerets (meaning 'abode of devils') is also the name of the quiet resort village lying below on the western approach to Col du Pillon.

Another steep meadow brings you to a junction of paths and a signpost by the farm of Schopfi (1502m, **45min**), perched on a hillside looking directly across the valley to yesterday's Krinnen Pass. Veer left on a vague grass path guided by marker posts which climbs through more pastures, still gaining height steeply but with fine views to compensate for the effort involved. About 30min from Schopfi you come to the cluster of farm buildings of Vorder Wallig (1725m, **1hr 30min**).

The route continues uphill a short distance to an upper track which you then follow along the hillside heading left, rising steadily, then contouring to the solitary alp of Topfelsberg (1801m). The track soon ends, to be replaced by a path which climbs to gain the panoramic saddle of the **Blattipass** (1918m, **2hr**). This grass- and shrub-covered ridge, punctuated with a few trees, has a truly memorable eastward view. ◀

Descend leftwards on the western side of the ridge, over grass slopes and dodging among groups of trees, with waymarks as an aid when the path is not evident on the ground. About 10min from the pass you come to the alp building of Ober Stuedli, with its views down to the Arnensee. A clear path now continues, descends among trees, then over pastures and across a pretty stream to join a track leading to the farm of **Seeberg** (1711m, **2hr 30min**). This occupies a charming site which also overlooks the Arnensee. There's a signed path junction here.

Leaving the farm below to your right, take the path climbing to Voré among alpenrose, juniper and bilberry. Larch and rowan stud the hillside, and at the head of the slope you go through a grassy col to enter a shallow pastureland basin unlike anything yet seen on the trail. Cross the basin above a small tarn and reach another path junction on the **Col de Voré** (1918m, **3hr 15min**). ▸

A drystone wall marks the boundary of cantons Bern and Vaud.

Bear right on the route to Col des Andérets, and in 5min pass Chalet Vieux (1949m, **3hr 45min**) where you now join a farm road. This gives a stretch of easy walking with more long views, and about 15min or so beyond Chalet Vieux you reach the **Col des Andérets** (2030m, **4hr 10min**) whose ridge carries the Rhône/Rhine watershed. Take a last look at the panorama of Oberland peaks; at Eiger, Blümlisalp, Wildstrubel, Les Diablerets; the splendid ripple of pastoral landscapes in between, and the gleaming Arnensee far below.

The Arnensee

Les Diablerets and the chalets of Isenau below Col des Andérets (Photo: Kev Reynolds)

As you swing round the hillside on the other side of the col, you realise that Montreux and Lac Léman cannot be so far away.

Once you cross the col it'll be the Dents du Midi that draws your focus. ◄

Losing height past ski-tows (with footpath short cuts), the road goes between the alp buildings of Chalets d'Isenau (1855m, refreshments). The way continues for a further 20min to reach **Le Resto d'Isenau** (1802m, **4hr 45min**, accommodation in beds and dormitories, refreshments, tel 024 492 32 93, www.isenau.ch) near the upper station of a gondola which comes from the resort of Les Diablerets.

At a junction of tracks here, take the path which cuts off to the right, signed to Chersaule and Col des Mosses. In truth it's not so much a path as a hint of previous walkers that guides you down the hillside to join a track leading to a lone farmhouse in a knuckle of the valley at 1686m. Passing the farm, cross a stream and continue along a path which makes a rising traverse of the north side of the valley, and in a further 30min comes to the alp hamlet of Meitreile (1803m).

The route from here to Col des Mosses is a truly scenic belvedere, the path remaining high above the valley

with fine views almost every step of the way. ▶ After 15min the way has descended a little to the Marnex (1738m) farm. Here you join a narrow, paved road that leads to a group of alp buildings at La Dix (1741m). Now you can see Mont Blanc to the left of the Dents du Midi, and all around (as ever) a great sweep of mountains and green valleys.

The road ends at La Dix, and a path continues, but shortly before reaching La Lé (1798m) you come onto another farm road which you follow for about 2km as far as the collection of farms and chalets of Chersaule (1655m). Leave the road here and climb to the right between the buildings and take a track through woodland, then out to a clearing on a spur of hillside near the farm of Oudiou (1702m, **7hr**).

Go through a gate on the right and descend half-left towards more woods and soon join a minor road. This traverses the hillside in woods, coming out into pastures from which Col des Mosses can be seen, passes small farm-chalets and close-shaved meadows, and finally brings you to the small resort of **Col des Mosses** (1439m, **8hr**).

There's still a long way to go, but it's a fairly regular contour with only a few minor ups and downs.

COL DES MOSSES (1439M)

A broad open plateau that acts as a major watershed at the head of two valley systems, the col has been developed as a small resort with several ski-tows on the western slopes, and a cableway rising in two stages to Pic Chaussy in the south-east. A popular outing from here visits the Lac Lioson, lying north-east of Pic Chaussy at 1848m.

Tourist information (tel 024 491 14 66, www.lesmosses.ch). Hotel, restaurants, shop, ATM, post office, bus connections with Château d'Oex and Le Sepey. Accommodation at: Hotel Le Relais Alpin (tel 024 491 05 00, www.leschaletsdesmosses.ch).

Col des Mosses link to Col de Sonlomont (Stage 18)
To connect from Col des Mosses to the Col de Sonlomont, head through the village and turn left off the road on Rt 46 through meadows and boggy ground (hence Les Mosses) and follow this to **La Lécherette**

Descending into Col des Mosses; it's normally a peaceful spot but the Sunday market changes this

(1379m, **1hr 10min**), turning right at the road near the entrance to a military camp and then left 10min later into and through the village. Follow the path between houses and then onto a road. Where the path turns right, keep on the road and steadily climb to join the route from Rossinière at the **Col de Sonlomont** (1501m, **2hr 30min**) (9.5km, 360m ascent, 300m descent). From here continue from the col – see Stage 18.

Note that a left turn along the road at La Lécherette will bring you to the **Vuichoude d'en Bas** junction (see Stage 18 map) in 3hr after 12.5km, all along the quiet road alongside the Lac de l'Hongrin, saving about 1hr against the Col de Sonlomont route.

APPENDIX A
Useful addresses

Tourist information

Details of tourist information offices in villages passed on the VA route are given in the text.

UK – Switzerland Travel Centre
Tel 44 (0) 207 420 4900
www.switzerlandtravelcentre.com

USA – Swiss National Tourist Office
tel 212 757 5944
www.myswitzerland.com

Map suppliers

Cordee Ltd
www.cordee.co.uk

Stanfords
www.stanfords.co.uk

The Map Shop
www.themapshop.co.uk

Omni Resources
www.omnimap.com

Swiss topographical maps are also available from national tourist offices and online.

Specialist mountain activities insurance

British Mountaineering Council Travel & Activity Insurance
www.thebmc.co.uk
BMC members only

Austrian Alpine Club
www.aacuk.org.uk
AAC membership carries accident and mountain rescue insurance plus reciprocal rights reductions in SAC huts.

Snowcard Insurance Services
www.snowcard.co.uk

Harrison Beaumont Ltd
tel 0345 450 8547
www.hbinsurance.co.uk

Organised treks on sections of the VA

Walkers' Britain (formerly Sherpa Expeditions)
www.walkersbritain.co.uk

Macs Adventure
www.macsadventure.com

Via Alpina stamping stations

Via Alpina hiking passbook
https://www.myswitzerland.com/en-ch/experiences/summer-autumn/hiking/via-alpina/
via-alpina-hiking-passbook/

Flight contacts

British Airways
www.britishairways.com

Swiss
www.swiss.com

Ryanair
www.ryanair.com

EasyJet
www.easyjet.com

Rail travel information

Eurostar
www.eurostar.com

Trainline
www.trainline.com

Rail Europe
www.raileurope.com

Swiss train timetables
www.sbb.ch

French railways
www.sncf.com

APPENDIX B
Bibliography

General tourist guides

The Rough Guide to Switzerland by Matthew Teller (Rough Guides). Perhaps the best and most readable of the many general guides available.

Switzerland by Gregor Clark, Craig McLachlan, Benedict Walker and Kerry Walker (Lonely Planet).

Mountain walking

The Swiss Alps by Kev Reynolds (Cicerone Press). Comprehensive coverage of all the mountain regions of Switzerland, with advice on all aspects of walking, trekking, climbing and skiing. Large sections are devoted to areas visited by the VA.

Walking in the Bernese Oberland – Jungfrau Region by Lesley Williams and Jonathan Williams (Cicerone Press). 50 day walks in Grindelwald, Wengen, Lauterbrunnen and Murren.

Trekking in the Alps edited by Kev Reynolds (Cicerone Press). Twenty classic trekking routes are described, including the VA.

Walking in the Alps by Kev Reynolds (Cicerone Press). All Alpine areas included, from the Alpes Maritime to the Julians of Slovenia, in 19 chapters. Plenty of coverage of areas visited on the VA.

Tour of the Jungfrau Region by Kev Reynolds (Cicerone Press). Ten days trekking in the Bernese Oberland.

APPENDIX C
German–French–English glossary

The following glossary contains a number of words likely to be found on maps, in village streets or in foreign-language tourist information leaflets. While it is not intended as a substitute for a pocket dictionary, it should be of some use.

German	French	English
Abfahrt	depart	departure
Abhang	pente	slope
Alp	haut pâturage	alp
Alpenblume	florealpe	alpine flower
Alpenverein	club alpin	alpine club
Alphütte	cabane, refuge	mountain hut
Ankunft	arrive	arrival
Ausgang	sortie	exit
Auskunft	renseignements	information
Aussischtspunkt	belle vue	viewpoint
Bach	ruisseau	stream, river
Bäckerei	boulangerie	bakery
Bahnhof	la gare	railway station
Berg	montagne	mountain
Bergführer	guide de montagne	mountain guide
Berggasthaus	hotel en haut	mountain inn
Bergpass	col	pass
Bergschrund	rimaye	crevasse between glacier and rock wall
Bergsteiger	alpiniste/grimpeur/-euse	mountaineer
Bergwanderer	randonneur/-euse	mountain walker
Bergweg	chemin de montagne	mountain path
Billet	billet	ticket
bitte	s'il vous plait	please
Blatt	feuille	map sheet

German	French	English
Brücke	*pont*	bridge
danke	*merci*	thank you
Dorf	*village*	village
Drahtseilbahn	*télépherique*	cable car
Ebene	*plaine, plan*	plain
Eingang	*entrée*	entrance
Feldweg	*chemin de terre*	meadowland path
Fels	*rocher*	rock wall
Ferienwohnung	*appartement de vacances*	holiday apartment
Flughafen	*aéroport*	airport
Fussweg	*sentier, chemin*	footpath
Garni	*garni*	hotel with breakfast only provided
Gasthaus/Gasthof	*auberge*	inn, guesthouse
Gaststube	*salon*	common room, lounge
gefährlich	*dangereux*	dangerous
Gemse	*chamois*	chamois
Geröllhalde	*éboulis*	scree
Gipfel	*sommet, cime*	summit, peak
Gletscher	*glacier*	glacier
Gletscherspalte	*crevasse*	crevasse
Gondelbahn	*télécabin*	gondola lift
Grat	*arête*	ridge
grüezi	*bonjour*	greetings
heiss	*chaud*	hot
Jugendherberge	*auberge de jeunesse*	youth hostel
kalt	*froid*	cold
Kamm	*crête*	crest, ridge
Kapelle	*chapelle*	chapel
Karte	*carte*	map

German	French	English
Kirche	église	church
Klamm	gorge, ravin	gorge
Klumme	combe	combe, small valley
Kurverein	office du tourisme	tourist office
Landschaft	paysage	landscape
Lawine	avalanche	avalanche
Lebensmittelgeschäft	épicerie	grocery
leicht	facile	easy
links	à gauche	left (direction)
Massenlager/ Matratzenlager	dortoir	dormitory
Moräne	moraine	moraine
Murmeltier	marmot	marmot
Nebel	brouillard	fog, low cloud, mist
nord	nord	north
ober	dessus	upper
ost	est	east
Pass	col	pass
Pension	pension	simple hotel
Pfad	sentier, chemin	path
Pickel	piolet	ice axe
Polizei	police	police
Quelle	source, fontaine	spring (of water)
rechts	à droite	right (direction)
Reh	roe	deer
Rucksack	sac à dos	rucksack
Ruhetag	jour de repos	day off
Sattel	selle	saddle, pass
Schlafraum	dortoir	bedroom
Schloss	château	castle
Schlucht	ravin, gorge	gorge

German	French	English
Schnee	*neige*	snow
See	*lac*	lake, tarn
Seil	*corde*	rope
Seilbahn	*télépherique*	cable car
Sesselbahn	*télésiège*	chairlift
Stausee	*reservoir*	reservoir
Steigesen	*crampons*	crampons
Steinmann	*cairn*	cairn
Steinschlag	*chute de pierres*	stonefall, falling rocks
Stunde(n)	*heure(s)*	hour(s)
sud	*sud*	south
Tal	*vallée*	valley
Tobel	*ravin boisé*	wooded ravine or gorge
Touristenlager	*dortoir*	dormitory, simple tourist accommodation
über	*via, par-dessus*	via, or over
Unfall	*accident*	accident
Unterkunft	*logement*	accommodation
Verkehrverein	*office (bureau) du tourisme*	tourist office
Wald	*forêt, bois*	forest, woodland
Wanderweg	*sentier, chemin*	footpath
warm	*chaud*	hot
Wasser	*eau*	water
Weide	*pâturage*	pasture
west	*ouest*	west
Wildbach	*torrent*	torrent
Zeltplatz	*camping*	campsite
Zimmer (frei)	*chambres (libre)*	bedroom (available)
Zug	*train*	train

APPENDIX D
Stage facilities planner

Stage	Place	Altitude (m)	Walking time	Cum. stage time
P	**Gaflei**	**1483**		
P	Vaduz	457	2hr 15min	2hr 15min
P	Azmoos	495	3hr 5min	5hr 20min
1	**Sargans**	**483**	**1hr 40min**	**7hr**
1	Mels	495	35min	35min
1	**Weisstannen**	**1004**	**3hr 25min**	**4hr**
2	Foopass	2223	4hr 45min	4hr 45min
2	**Elm**	**979**	**2hr 45min**	**7hr 30min**
3	Obererbs	1703	3hr 15min	3hr 15min
3	Richetlipass	2261	2hr 15min	5hr 30min
3	**Linthal**	**650**	**3hr 15min**	**8hr 45min**
4	Braunwald	1256	1hr 45min	1hr 45min
4	**Urnerboden**	**1383**	**3hr 45min**	**5hr 30min**
5	Klausenpass	1948	2hr 15min	2hr 15min
5	Urigen	1280	3hr 15min	5hr 30min
5	Spirigen	970	45min	6hr 15min
5	**Altdorf**	**458**	**2hr 15min**	**8hr 30min**
6	Attinghausen	490	45min	45min
6	Brüsti	1528	3hr	3hr 45min
6	Surenenpass	2292	2hr 30min	6hr 15min
6	Blacklenalp	1769	1hr	7hr 15min
6	Stäfeli	1393	1hr	8hr 15min
6	**Engelberg**	**1000**	**2hr 15min**	**10hr 30min**

Legend: ◯ hotel ⬆ mountain hut/inn ⬡ campsite 🍴 refreshments ⊕ shop ▣ train station ▣ bus service 🚠 cable car ℹ information

Distance (km)	Cum. stage distance (km)	Hotel	Hut	Campsite	Refreshments	Shop	Bus	Train	Cable car	Info
		◯			🍴			▣		
8.2	8.2	◯		⬡	🍴	⊕		▣		ℹ
12.3	20.5	◯			🍴	⊕		▣		
6.5	**27**	◯		⬡	🍴	⊕	▣	▣		ℹ
2.5	2.5	◯			🍴	⊕		▣		
11.0	**13.5**	◯			🍴			▣		
13.3	13.3									
9.7	**23.0**	◯		⬡	🍴	⊕		▣	🚠	ℹ
10.0	10.0		⬆					▣		
5.1	15.1									
9.4	**24.5**	◯		⬡	🍴	⊕	▣	▣	🚠	ℹ
4.2	4.2	◯			🍴	⊕			🚠	
13.3	**17.5**	◯			🍴	⊕		▣		
6.0	6.0	◯			🍴			▣		
10.8	16.8	◯			🍴			▣		
2.7	19.5	◯			🍴	⊕		▣		
8.5	**28.0**	◯		⬡	🍴	⊕	▣	▣		ℹ
3.6	3.6	◯						▣	🚠	
4.4	8.0		⬆		🍴				🚠	
6	14.0									
3	17.0		⬆							
3.5	20.5		⬆							
9	**29.5**	◯		⬡	🍴	⊕	▣	▣	🚠	ℹ

TREKKING THE SWISS VIA ALPINA

Stage	Place	Altitude (m)	Walking time	Cum. stage time	
7	Trübsee	1788	2hr 30min	2hr 30min	
7	Jochpass	2208	1hr 30min	4hr	
7	**Engstlenalp**	**1835**	**1hr**	**5hr**	
8	Tannalp	1976	0hr 50min	50min	
8	Planplatten	2229	2hr 40min	3hr 30min	
8	Reuti	1065	2hr 30min	6hr	
8	**Meiringen**	**600**	**1hr**	**7hr**	
9	Rosenlaui	1328	3hr	3hr	
9	Grosse Scheidegg	1962	2hr 30min	5hr 30min	
9	**Grindelwald**	**1040**	**2hr 30min**	**8hr**	
10	Alpiglen	1616	2hr 15min	2hr 15min	
10	Kleine Scheidegg	2061	1hr 30min	3hr 45min	
10	Wengen	1276	1hr 45min	5hr 30min	
10	**Lauterbrunnen**	**800**	**1hr**	**6hr 30min**	
11	Mürren	1638	2hr 30min	2hr 30min	
11	Rotstock Hut	2039	2hr 15min	4hr 45min	
11	Sefinafurgga	2611	1hr 30min	6hr 15min	
11	**Griesalp**	**1408**	**3hr**	**9hr 15min**	
12	Oberi Bundalp	1841	1hr 15min	1hr 15min	
12	Hohtürli/Blümlisalp Hut	2837	2hr 45min	4hr	
12	Oeschinensee	1593	2hr 30min	6hr 30min	
12	**Kandersteg**	**1170**	**1hr**	**7hr 30min**	
13	Bunderchrinde	2382	4hr	4hr	
13	Bonderalp	1755	1hr 20min	5hr 20min	
13	**Adelboden**	**1350**	**1hr 40min**	**7hr**	
14	Hahnenmoospass	1950	2hr 45min	2hr 45min	
14	**Lenk**	**1064**	**1hr 45min**	**4hr 30min**	

204

Distance (km)	Cum. stage distance (km)	Facilities								
5.0	5.0	○		◬	🍴				🚡	
3.1	8.1		▲						🚡	
3.9	**12.0**	○						◉		
2.7	2.7		▲							
8.2	10.9				🍴				🚡	
7.8	18.7	○			🍴	⊕		◉	🚡	
3.8	**22.5**	○		◬	🍴	⊕	◼	◉	🚡	ⓘ
7.9	7.9	○						◉		
6.7	14.6		▲							
8.4	**23.0**	○		◬	🍴	⊕	◼	◉	🚡	ⓘ
5.3	5.3		▲					◉		
4.3	9.6	○	▲		🍴			◉		
6.9	16.5	○			🍴	⊕	◼		🚡	
3.0	**19.5**	○		◬	🍴	⊕	◼	◉	🚡	ⓘ
6.0	6.0	○			🍴	⊕	◼		🚡	ⓘ
6.3	12.3		▲							
3.1	15.4									
7.1	**22.5**	○	▲					◉		
2.8	2.8		▲							
4	6.8		▲							
5.9	12.7	○	▲		🍴				🚡	
5.3	**18.0**	○		◬	🍴	⊕	◼	◉	🚡	ⓘ
9.2	9.2									
3	12.2		▲							
5.3	**17.5**	○			🍴	⊕		◉	🚡	ⓘ
8.5	8.5		▲						🚡	
5.5	**14.0**	○		◬	🍴	⊕	◼	◉	🚡	ⓘ

Stage	Place	Altitude (m)	Walking time	Cum. stage time
15	Trütlisbergpass	2037	3hr 30min	3hr 30min
15	**Gstaad**	**1050**	**3hr 30min**	**7hr**
16	Col de Jable	1883	4hr 45min	4hr 45min
16	**L'Etivaz**	**1140**	**1hr 45min**	**6hr 30min**
17	Chateau d'Oex	958	2hr 30min	2hr 30min
17	**Rossinière**	**918**	**1hr 30min**	**4hr**
18	Col de Sonlomont	1501	2hr 30min	2hr 30min
18	**Rochers de Naye**	**1971**	**5hr 30min**	**8hr**
19	Caux	1048	2hr	2hr
19	**Montreux**	**370**	**2hr**	**4hr**
Alternative finish				
15A	**Lenk**	**1064**		
15A	Trütlisbergpass	2037	3hr 30min	3hr 30min
15A	Lauenen	1240	1hr 50min	5hr 20min
15A	**Gsteig**	**1183**	**2hr 40min**	**8hr**
16A	**Col des Mosses**	**1439**	**8hr**	**8hr**
18	**Rochers de Naye**	**1971**	**8hr**	**8hr**
19	Caux	1048	2hr	2hr
19	**Montreux**	**370**	**2hr**	**4hr**

Distance (km)	Cum. stage distance (km)	Facilities							
8.5	8.5								
14.0	**22.5**	○	△	🍴	⊕	▣	▣	🚐	ℹ
10.9	10.9								
5.6	**16.5**	○		🍴			▣		
9.0	9.0	○		🍴	⊕	▣	▣		ℹ
5.5	**14.5**	○			⊕	▣			
6.1	6.1								
12.9	**19.0**	○		🍴		▣			
8.2	8.2	○		🍴		▣			
5.8	**14.0**	○	△	🍴	⊕	▣	▣		ℹ
		○	△	🍴	⊕	▣	▣	🚐	ℹ
8.5	8.5								
6.7	15.2	○	△	🍴	⊕		▣		
7.3	**22.5**	○			⊕		▣		
25.0	**25.0**	○	△	🍴	⊕		▣		
22.5	**22.5**	○		🍴		▣			
8.2	8.2	○		🍴		▣			
5.8	**14.0**	○	△	🍴	⊕	▣	▣		ℹ

NOTES

NOTES

DOWNLOAD THE ROUTES
IN GPX FORMAT

All the routes in this guide are available for download from:

www.cicerone.co.uk/1160/GPX

as standard format GPX files. You should be able to load them into most online GPX systems and mobile devices, whether GPS or smartphone. You may need to convert the file into your preferred format using a conversion programme such as gpsvisualizer.com or one of the many other such websites and programmes.

When you follow this link, you will be asked for your email address and where you purchased the guidebook, and have the option to subscribe to the Cicerone e-newsletter.

www.cicerone.co.uk

LISTING OF CICERONE GUIDES

BRITISH ISLES CHALLENGES, COLLECTIONS AND ACTIVITIES

Cycling Land's End to John o' Groats
Great Walks on the England Coast Path
The Big Rounds
The Book of the Bivvy
The Book of the Bothy
The Mountains of England & Wales:
  Vol 1 Wales
  Vol 2 England
The National Trails
Walking the End to End Trail

SHORT WALKS SERIES

Short Walks Hadrian's Wall
Short Walks in Arnside and Silverdale
Short Walks in Dumfries and Galloway
Short Walks in Nidderdale
Short Walks in the Lake District:
  Windermere Ambleside and Grasmere
Short Walks on the Malvern Hills
Short Walks in the Surrey Hills
Short Walks Winchester

SCOTLAND

Ben Nevis and Glen Coe
Cycle Touring in Northern Scotland
Cycling in the Hebrides
Great Mountain Days in Scotland
Mountain Biking in Southern and Central Scotland
Mountain Biking in West and North West Scotland
Not the West Highland Way Scotland
Scotland's Best Small Mountains
Scotland's Mountain Ridges
Scottish Wild Country Backpacking
Skye's Cuillin Ridge Traverse
The Borders Abbeys Way
The Great Glen Way
The Great Glen Way Map Booklet
The Hebridean Way
The Hebrides
The Isle of Mull
The Isle of Skye
The Skye Trail
The Southern Upland Way
The West Highland Way
The West Highland Way Map Booklet
Walking Ben Lawers, Rannoch and Atholl
Walking in the Cairngorms
Walking in the Pentland Hills
Walking in the Scottish Borders
Walking in the Southern Uplands

Walking in Torridon, Fisherfield, Fannichs and An Teallach
Walking Loch Lomond and the Trossachs
Walking on Arran
Walking on Harris and Lewis
Walking on Jura, Islay and Colonsay
Walking on Rum and the Small Isles
Walking on the Orkney and Shetland Isles
Walking on Uist and Barra
Walking the Cape Wrath Trail
Walking the Corbetts
  Vol 1 South of the Great Glen
  Vol 2 North of the Great Glen
Walking the Galloway Hills
Walking the John o' Groats Trail
Walking the Munros
  Vol 1 – Southern, Central and Western Highlands
  Vol 2 – Northern Highlands and the Cairngorms
Winter Climbs: Ben Nevis and Glen Coe

NORTHERN ENGLAND ROUTES

Cycling the Reivers Route
Cycling the Way of the Roses
Hadrian's Cycleway
Hadrian's Wall Path
Hadrian's Wall Path Map Booklet
The Coast to Coast Cycle Route
The Coast to Coast Walk
The Coast to Coast Walk Map Booklet
The Pennine Way
The Pennine Way Map Booklet
Walking the Dales Way
Walking the Dales Way Map Booklet

NORTH-EAST ENGLAND, YORKSHIRE DALES AND PENNINES

Cycling in the Yorkshire Dales
Great Mountain Days in the Pennines
Mountain Biking in the Yorkshire Dales
The Cleveland Way and the Yorkshire Wolds Way
The Cleveland Way Map Booklet
The North York Moors
The Reivers Way
Trail and Fell Running in the Yorkshire Dales
Walking in County Durham
Walking in Northumberland
Walking in the North Pennines
Walking in the Yorkshire Dales: North and East
Walking in the Yorkshire Dales: South and West

Walking St Cuthbert's Way
Walking St Oswald's Way and Northumberland Coast Path

NORTH-WEST ENGLAND AND THE ISLE OF MAN

Cycling the Pennine Bridleway
Isle of Man Coastal Path
The Lancashire Cycleway
The Lune Valley and Howgills
Walking in Cumbria's Eden Valley
Walking in Lancashire
Walking in the Forest of Bowland and Pendle
Walking on the Isle of Man
Walking on the West Pennine Moors
Walking the Ribble Way
Walks in Silverdale and Arnside

LAKE DISTRICT

Bikepacking in the Lake District
Cycling in the Lake District
Great Mountain Days in the Lake District
Joss Naylor's Lakes, Meres and Waters of the Lake District
Lake District Winter Climbs
Lake District:
  High Level and Fell Walks
Lake District:
  Low Level and Lake Walks
Mountain Biking in the Lake District
Outdoor Adventures with Children – Lake District
Scrambles in the Lake District – North
Scrambles in the Lake District – South
Trail and Fell Running in the Lake District
Walking The Cumbria Way
Walking the Lake District Fells –
  Borrowdale
  Buttermere
  Coniston
  Keswick
  Langdale
  Mardale and the Far East
  Patterdale
  Wasdale
Walking the Tour of the Lake District

DERBYSHIRE, PEAK DISTRICT AND MIDLANDS

Cycling in the Peak District
Dark Peak Walks
Scrambles in the Dark Peak
Walking in Derbyshire
Walking in the Peak District – White Peak East
Walking in the Peak District – White Peak West

For full information on all our
guides, books and eBooks,
visit our website:
www.cicerone.co.uk

CICERONE

Trust Cicerone to guide your next adventure, wherever it may be around the world...

Discover guides for hiking, mountain walking, backpacking, trekking, trail running, cycling and mountain biking, ski touring, climbing and scrambling in Britain, Europe and worldwide.

Connect with Cicerone online and find inspiration.

- buy books and ebooks
- articles, advice and trip reports
- podcasts and live events
- GPX files and updates
- regular newsletter

cicerone.co.uk